This is the book I have missed! You know that you have missed some books, the first time you read them. For me this is such a book. From my experiences of having worked as a middle leader for teacher development for the last two decades, I am more convinced than ever that for professional and school-based development to be sustained means recognising the interplay between teachers' past, present and the future practices. This means that professionals, like middle leaders, need methods, models and theories that help them to develop the competencies needed to do this work. This guidance and support is presented in this book.

Dr Lisbeth Gyllander Torkildsen, Director of Quality and Development Department, Malmö, Sweden

Middle leaders are the silent, at times overlooked leaders and administrators of professional learning and classroom practice. This book places them at the centre of the action in schools, as agents of professional learning who lead practice through action research. They are the players and the risk takers. This book is rich with vignettes that provide us with the evidence of practice we need as researchers and practitioners to celebrate the importance of middle leading in the life of the school. Unpacking these rich examples of practice using the theory of practice architectures, with additional resources, Grootenboer, Edwards-Groves and Rönnerman show us how and why middle leading matters, and what to do next.

Dr Christine Grice, Christine Grice, Lecturer, Educational Leadership Sydney School of Education and Social Work, The University of Sydney, Australia

Middle Leadership in Schools

Middle leading refers to those teachers that both teach and have leadership roles, and thus can bridge the gap between the practices of learning and the management of schooling. Focusing on the practices of middle leaders, this book addresses the current lack of support and professional development for middle leaders in educational settings.

Middle Leadership in Schools positions middle leaders as professional leaders, and an integral part of educational and professional development in schools and other educational institutions. Drawing on empirical research spanning four countries, this book provides readers with a conceptual framework to understand middle leading and shows how middle leading practices unfold in real educational contexts. This is a valuable resource that goes beyond a theoretical conversation about middle leaders to provide readers with practical applications based on extensive research undertaken by the authors. The book is divided into seven chapters, each of which include reflective discussion questions and recommended readings to promote collaborative engagement with the text. Chapters cover topics such as how middle leading is shaped in practice, its role in professional development and its impact on schools.

Illustrating to middle leaders how they can develop their leadership skills, the book will also be of interest to school principals and other senior leaders as a guide to supporting their middle leaders.

Peter Grootenboer was a school teacher and middle leader for 12 years before moving into the tertiary sector. He received a national Jim Campbell Award for teaching excellence. He is now a Professor in Education at Griffith University.

Christine Edwards-Groves is Associate Professor at Charles Sturt University, Australia. She researches classroom interaction, dialogic pedagogies, and professional learning, and is especially interested in practice theory.

Karin Rönnerman is a Professor in Education at the University of Gothenburg. Her research is in the field of action research connected to professional learning and development of practices through middle leading.

Middle Leadership in Schools
A Practical Guide for Leading Learning

Peter Grootenboer, Christine Edwards-Groves and Karin Rönnerman

LONDON AND NEW YORK

First published 2020
by Routledge
2 Park Square, Milton Park, Abingdon, Oxon OX14 4RN

and by Routledge
52 Vanderbilt Avenue, New York, NY 10017

Routledge is an imprint of the Taylor & Francis Group, an informa business

© 2020 Peter Grootenboer, Christine Edwards-Groves, Karin Rönnerman

The right of Peter Grootenboer, Christine Edwards-Groves, Karin Rönnerman to be identified as authors of this work has been asserted by them in accordance with sections 77 and 78 of the Copyright, Designs and Patents Act 1988.

All rights reserved. No part of this book may be reprinted or reproduced or utilised in any form or by any electronic, mechanical, or other means, now known or hereafter invented, including photocopying and recording, or in any information storage or retrieval system, without permission in writing from the publishers.

Trademark notice: Product or corporate names may be trademarks or registered trademarks, and are used only for identification and explanation without intent to infringe.

British Library Cataloguing-in-Publication Data
A catalogue record for this book is available from the British Library

Library of Congress Cataloging-in-Publication Data
A catalog record has been requested for this book

ISBN: 978-0-367-45998-7 (hbk)
ISBN: 978-0-367-46000-6 (pbk)
ISBN: 978-1-003-02638-9 (ebk)

Typeset in Bembo
by Taylor & Francis Books
Printed and bound by CPI Group (UK) Ltd, Croydon CR0 4YY

Contents

List of illustrations — viii
Acknowledgements — ix
Foreword — xi
Leading from the middle: words from a middle leader — xiv

1. Leading from the middle — 1
2. Practices and practice architectures of middle leading — 18
3. School-based professional learning and development — 38
4. Relating, trust, and dialogic practice in middle leading — 49
5. Evidence-informed development — 77
6. Middle leading in practice — 93
7. Middle leading as a practice-changing practice — 109

Appendix 1: Facilitating teacher reflection: questions and strategies — 123
Appendix 2: Interactive strategies for facilitating focused reflection, rich discussion, and critical thinking — 130
Appendix 3: Questions to guide evidentiary talk in professional learning conversations and for individual self-reflection — 140
Appendix 4: Conversation transcription conventions — 143
Appendix 5: Supporting a dialogic approach: an example from the field – teacher reflection questions — 144
Appendix 6: Learning together through action-oriented professional learning: a guide to collaborative peer coaching in the classroom setting — 146
Index — 150

Illustrations

Figures

1.1	Positioning of the middle leader	9
2.1	The education complex of practices	20
2.2	The centrality of middle leading for school formation and transformation	21
2.3	Interrelationships between 'changing' technological practices and teacher professional development	24
2.4	Projects as constituted by practices as constituted by sayings, doings, and relatings	27
2.5	Y chart	36
3.1	Basic action research cycles	40
5.1	Simple recording equipment	87
5.2	Camera (iPad) stand set-up	88

Tables

1.1	Examples of middle leading roles and not middle leading roles	3
4.1	Interpersonal trust	50
4.2	Interactional trust	51
4.3	Intersubjective trust	52
4.4	Intellectual trust	53
4.5	Pragmatic trust	53

Acknowledgements

To the middle leaders, the educators invested in educating their peers *and* their own students in classrooms, and with whom we have worked for some decades now – sincere thanks is extended for sharing your practices. Your work is critical for site-based education development in every classroom, in every school, in every community, in every nation across the globe. As Keith Basso so rightly reminds us – *wisdom sits in places* – your wisdom inspires and teaches us about the enduring need to begin in and be responsive to sites.

We especially thank Kirsten Petrie and Deana Gray for their generous and wise spirit in the words that open this book.

We openly and sincerely thank our 'middle leading' research colleagues – Kirsten Petrie and Tess Boyle – for their collaborative work on educational leadership over the last few years. Also, we would like to express our gratitude for the continuous support, partnership with, and recognition from our PEP colleagues in Australia, New Zealand, Sweden, Norway, Colombia, and Finland.

Peter would like to first, acknowledge the on-going love and support of his family – Ange, Jake, Tilly, Danneke, Mikey, Willem, Beverley, Matthew, Janine, and Michelle. He would also like to thank his colleagues at Griffith University including Katherine Tucker, Tracey Morris, Julia McMath, Sarah Buckler, Alex Smith, Kane Bradford, Thea Anderson, and Alexandra Laird. Finally, Peter expresses his sincere appreciation for other colleagues who have worked with him on projects related to middle leadership, including Sharon Tindall, Kylie Lipscombe, Catherine Attard, Christine Grice, Larissa Maraga and Pieta Lack.

Christine takes her hat off to the teachers and middle leaders with whom she has worked – your practices have shaped and reshaped her thinking and scholarship for well over three decades – thank you. She particularly thanks her colleagues Christina Davidson (Charles Sturt University), and Michele Anstey and Geoff Bull (ABC Consulting), who in recent action research collaborations focused on developing dialogic pedagogies have been instrumental in keeping the core business of collegiality, dialogue, and intellectual debate alive. Her good friend Stephen Kemmis once wrote '*we live our life in practices*', and with this Christine appreciates and recognises the academic friendship with long time co-authors and research collaborators Peter and Karin and what this means for living a scholarly life. Last, but by no means least, she thanks the unconditional support given by her family in this crazy business called academia.

Karin would like to acknowledge all teachers enrolled in courses or in collaborations about action research. These teachers have willingly been sharing their experiences with her in dialogues, taken time to be interviewed and sometimes let her in to their classrooms. All this have meant much in understanding the field of professional learning and development. She is also grateful for her colleagues in the research group she is a leader of at the University of Gothenburg. Their comments and support in acting as critical friends have been important in sharing ideas and in the writing processes. Last she wants to thank Christine and Peter for productive and creative years in collaboration where academic work is pure joy.

Foreword

Educational leadership resources (books, articles, professional learning opportunities) typically focus on the leading from the top, the front. These resources speak to 'principals'[1]; and in doing so, neglect to provide theoretical and practical resources for other leaders in 'school' (or other educational) settings. Those that lead from the middle, whose practice of leading occurs between the principal's leadership and the pedagogical practices of classroom teachers, have not previously been well catered for. That is until now.

In this book, *Middle Leadership: Leading Professional Learning,* the authors establish a clear and engaging argument for the important role of middle leaders. Often neglected in a world of rhetoric associated with school leadership, or in the abundance of resources developed associated with leading and professional learning, the authors of this book sophisticatedly demonstrate the unique position of middle leaders in education contexts. As is so elegantly argued in this book, it is the middle leader, and less frequently the principal, who are best positioned to impact on the core business of teaching and leading in school. It is this positionality, sandwiched in the middle, that allow those leading in the middle to 'bridge the educational work of classrooms and the management practices of administrators/leaders' (Grootenboer, Edwards-Groves and Rönnerman, 2014, p. 509), through the sophisticated and effective collegial relationships and collaborative leading practices. The accessibility of this text consolidates the significant role middle leaders play in developing practices that enhance their own and colleagues learning (and teaching, professional learning, and leading), and subsequently the learning experiences and outcomes for students.

At the same time, the authors strongly advocate for the use of evidence to help inform a process of morally informed educational change. As they focus on importance of gathering evidence, in multiple forms, to help teachers examine: What is happening here?, How has this change impacted teaching and how has this impacted learning?, the authors encourage a shift from a focus on data, as a form of statistical measurement, to data as evidence for informing practice and practice development. This much more holistic approach to considering evidence and the important role it plays in the core business of education, focuses the reader on professional learning for themselves and, at the same time, building the middle leader's knowledge about supporting others develop their teaching practices. This move comes from practice informed by what is happening in the site of the classrooms and local contexts.

Not happy to settle for illuminating the important place and contribution of middle leaders, the authors: Grootenboer, Edwards-Groves, and Rönnerman, provide a brilliantly constructed text, developed to assist middle leaders to lead school-based professional learning in ways that embed cultures of practice that change educational practice as curriculum and pedagogy. In their rich and descriptive writing approach, they make a strong statement about the need for site-based localised professional learning and educational development through action research, and how these ways of working can be central to teacher learning practices in school settings. The use of action research as a model for teacher learning and enhancing practices challenges to the reader to move beyond promoting or leading professional learning as a series of 'quick fix', one-off episodes. At the same time, the vignettes – stories from practice – embedded in each chapter offer insights in to the use of action research as a mechanism to hand the learning to the learner by supporting the middle leaders leading and learning practices of teachers in a range of educational settings. These narrative accounts consolidate key points and theoretical perspectives, whilst providing rich 'practical' examples of how other practitioners in education have utilised a range of strategies to maximise their own learning and to support the professional learning of others. Framed in relation to processes, techniques, and strategies the book in its entirety succeeds in presenting multiple cases of how middle leaders, and the authors, have worked to structure, negotiate and normalise action research for practice change, without creating a workload burden for colleagues.

Advocated throughout the book is that sustainable change, while it takes time, needs to be localised. Although experienced as slow, this approach lends itself to more enjoyable and meaningful learning for teachers and students. The notion of *playing in the sandpit* legitimises this idea; this reminds middle leaders, and those they work with, about how essential it is to take time to practise new practices, try out ideas, take risks, challenge and critique current practice, flesh out ideas, test new programmes, and generally 'play' with practice and work with evidence in response to the changing needs of their students and the context of their classes.

The accessible style of the writing in *Middle Leadership: Leading Professional Learning* makes it easy to imagine colleagues in education settings engrossed in the vignettes, considering how they develop relational trust and dialogic approaches that open communicative spaces, and actually rehearsing their repertoires of dialogic talk moves. These examples show how middle leaders practise – springing from the desire to enhance their own learning, that of their colleagues and the learning experiences of their students. Grootenboer, Edwards-Groves, and Rönnerman, in the way they have presented the theory and practice examples, model the generosity of middle leaders in the theory-practice balance by providing some provocations and starting points, but avoiding giving the formulaic recipe. In doing so they respect the professionalism and capabilities of middle leaders, as educators who can draw from concepts and examples provided and reshape these for the context specific needs of their own education site, and specific needs of that school community.

The significance of this exceptional book lies in the insightful recognition of the role middle leaders play as key agents in professional learning and the development of a professional learning culture. The strength of both the theoretical arguments coupled with practice-based evidence lends this book to being a formative text and compulsory read for everyone in education who is currently or who aspires to lead professional learning as localised site-based practice. It would be my utmost hope that practices advocated for in *Middle Leadership: Leading Professional Learning* become infused across school settings, as what is presented is an accessible platform for reconsidering how we currently think and practise leading and professional learning in school settings.

Kirsten Petrie
Te Huataki Waiora School of Health
The University of Waikato

Note

1 The positional head of a school or early years educational setting.

Leading from the middle: words from a middle leader

I can't play tennis....

Yet.

Let me explain, I grew up in a small country town in rural Australia. After school and on weekends I spent a lot of time with my friends, all of whom played multiple sports – including tennis. At various times I would attempt to play too, however I found it extremely difficult. And I was extremely bad at it.

Fast forward almost three decades, and you will now see me every Friday afternoon at tennis coaching with my husband and three children. We decided that learning to play would be a great way to spend time together, and although I knew my previous attempts at the game were woeful, my desire to get better and be with my family outweighed my reservations.

Surprisingly, I am improving at a faster rate than any of us had anticipated, and I am proud to say I now have a rather menacing forehand and a backhand that often goes over the net! I know that there are a lot of factors that are going into my improvement – I am growth-minded, I have motivation, I have the right equipment, and the psychological support of people that are important to me. I also have an extraordinary coach. And it is this final component that has played such a pivotal role in my improvement. Without his excellence in teaching, my *will* and my *opportunity* to play may never have actually resulted in any change in my *learning* and *progress*.

As I read the manuscript for *Middle Leadership: Leading Professional Learning*, my current experience as a student came to mind along with one of the most significant and widely recognised understandings within our current educational landscape – excellence in teaching has the most powerful influence on achievement. In knowing the profound impact of teachers who make a difference, the authors of this text have unambiguously centralised the importance of those within classrooms and the pivotal ways in which it is the classroom teacher who enacts the initiatives, policies, directives, and research of those who reside within different, yet interdependent, educational spaces. Specifically, they look to the role of **middle leaders** – those who hold a *leadership position* and *classroom teaching* responsibilities.

Grootenboer, Edwards-Groves and Rönnerman outline ways that middle leading is about *generative pedagogical leadership* driven through site-based and evidence-informed professional learning. Throughout their exploration of this influential role, they weave together both theoretical and practical insights via a range of case studies and vignettes. The power of these insights spring to life when the words of middle leaders themselves are framed, which again gives rise to those who choose for their educational contribution to be centred around their own work in classrooms and the unique opportunity they have to impact richly on their teaching colleagues – through their middle leading.

Throughout, the work of the middle leader is viewed through a praxis-informed lens, and is theorised by way of an intelligent and thought-provoking exploration of *ecologies of practice* and *practice architectures*. As part of this, the authors espouse how practices such as action research can provide a pathway for deep thinking and inquiry. They often draw from the substantial body of work from Kemmis *et al.*, who articulately frames the significance of an inward-facing focus by stating, in teacher action research 'we do not aim to produce generalisations about the "one best way" to do things. In fact, we don't want to find the best way to do things anywhere *except* here – where we are, in our situation' (2014, p. 69).

In order to support middle leaders with their 'practice-changing practice', an emphasis on the collaborative and communicative aspects of leadership is explored. As part of this, the elements of *relational trust* are rightly regarded as the cornerstone for pedagogical transformation, and the sustained commitment that is needed to achieve educational goals. Through the authors' rich research and educational practice over several decades, they expertly provide guidance, a roadmap of sorts, on strategic ways for middle leaders to be critical agents in facilitating responsive and deliberative learning in their schools. Importantly, they also direct our attention to the significance of measuring impact through understanding 'recognisably worthwhile' evidence. For what good is all of this if we do not seek to have insight into the *how, what*, and *why* of our morally-driven, professional endeavours?

As a middle leader myself, I have found the insights provided in *Middle Leading: Leading Professional Learning* powerful, due to the grounded way in which it is based on the everyday landscapes of schools, as well as the way it champions classroom-based leaders. This leads me to end where I began, with knowing and extending that:

> teachers make a difference –
> and those who **lead-*and*-teach** can make the biggest difference of all.

Deana Gray
Middle leader
Red Hill Public School, Wagga Wagga
NSW Department of Education, NSW, Australia

References

Grootenboer, P., Edwards-Groves and Rönnerman, K. (2014). 'Leading practice development: Voices from the middle', *Professional Development in Education*, 41(3), 508–526.

Kemmis, S., Wilkinson, J., Edwards-Groves, C., Hardy, I., Grootenboer, P. and Bristol, L. (2014). *Changing Practices, Changing Education*. Singapore: Springer.

1 Leading from the middle

Introduction

Leadership matters in education, and it matters at all levels and in all domains. We have known for a long time that leadership is important in education, and that good leadership is a critical factor in successful schooling. This assertion is grounded in almost half a century of research into educational leadership from across a range of countries and continents. However, while there is a plethora of literature on educational leadership, almost all of it is about principals and positional heads. But we know that in schools, and other educational institutions, leadership is not just the prerogative of the principal – there are many others who are leading the education in the school. It is these leaders who we want to address in this book, and to think about how their leading practices can be understood and developed. We describe these leaders as 'middle leaders'. In the past *middle leaders* have not received as much attention in development and research forums, but their work in schools, with teachers, with students, and with principals are critical to the provision and development of education in schools, early childhood centres, vocational training colleges, and other educational institutions. It seems to us that middle leaders are generally offered little professional development, training, or support for their roles, and so here we want to provide some ideas that can fill that gap.

In this book we consider middle leaders as key agents in leading professional learning – curriculum and pedagogical development. They have an acknowledged position of responsibility in the school but they are also still practising as teachers in the classroom, and as a consequence of this work they are well-placed to understand and develop the core business of schooling – learning (here we mean both teacher learning and student learning). This is a role that is not as open to the principal because they are somewhat distant from the classroom; nor is it available to a classroom teacher alone who does not have the resources available to those in more leadership positions. Also, we do not think that we can simply use or apply the models and concepts that have been developed for principal's leadership (e.g. distributed leadership) to understand the practices of middle leaders: they are fundamentally different. Middle leading requires a different kind of educational leadership. Therefore, in this book we want to specifically help middle leaders to understand their practices and roles, and to help them develop in their professions, because we believe that they are critical for 'good' education.

Before we move on, perhaps it is important to clarify a few terms:

- In this book we will usually use the term 'school', but we mean all forms of educational institutions – e.g. early childhood centres, primary schools, elementary schools, middle schools, secondary schools, vocational colleges, and university schools and faculties.
- Also, we often use the generic term 'classroom', but here we mean any site where formal learning and teaching occurs. This includes outdoor spaces, gymnasiums, laboratories, workshops, and even virtual and online spaces.
- We also will commonly use the term 'principal' to refer to the positional head of a school, noting that in different contexts these people may have different titles (e.g. headmaster, head of school, etc.).
- Finally, we will often refer to 'leading' rather than 'leadership', and this is a deliberate attempt to focus on the practices of leaders (what they are doing, saying and how they are relating to others), rather than their positions or personal qualities per se. This idea will be discussed further in Chapter 2.

Of course, the key term we need to define here is 'middle leader'; next we take some time to outline and discuss this important dimension of educational leading.

Who are middle leaders?

The terms 'middle leader' and 'middle leading' have recently become a little more prominent in systemic and educational rhetoric, and have been used to refer to two broad groups of practitioners. Hargreaves and Ainscow (2015) and Fullan (2015) use the term 'middle leaders' to refer to leading work undertaken at a regional level in large-scale reforms, while others direct its meaning towards middle management. This is where we differ. From our position, when we refer to middle leaders, we are referring to leaders in schools that have both an acknowledged **leadership** position AND some **teaching** responsibilities. We define it this way:

> It is middle leaders who have some positional (and/or acknowledged) responsibility to bring about change in their schools, yet maintain close connections to the classroom as sites where student learning occurs. In one sense, middle leaders bridge the educational practices of 'classrooms' and the management practices of the administrators/leaders.
> (Grootenboer, Edwards-Groves and Rönnerman, 2014, p. 509)

The critical point of difference in our thinking is that these education professionals, middle leaders, both *lead* and *teach* (students). This means for us, that middle leaders may have assorted titles and positions depending on the nature, type, size, and context of the school. In Table 1.1 below we outline some of the roles that could be considered as middle leaders, and ones that are not.

Although we offer these roles as examples, we are equally aware that the nature of the work of 'middle leaders' will vary depending on the size, structures, and organisational arrangements in different schools. In a very large school, the principal and several deputy principals may not have any regular teaching roles in the classroom, and therefore, they would not be middle leaders. However, in a smaller school, it may be that all the deputy principals also have a substantial teaching workload, and so they would be considered as middle leaders under our definition. Principals in rural and remote schools differ again since in their unique position they both have systemic leadership (management and administration) responsibilities *and* have a substantial teaching role, and so, in these circumstances may actually be considered a middle leader.

What we are clear on is that we are not talking about *middle management*, as this term for us has particular meanings and connotations that we are trying to avoid (ones often related to business models of education). As middle leader, Peita Lack, explained to us after she thought about how to develop her own middle leading practices:

> The first thing I needed to do was to know who I was, and what my leadership style was. I knew I was good at what I did. I paid attention to detail, I worked in an orderly, conscientious way. I am task orientated and I strive to make astute decisions. But this was not leadership… this was management. So my first realisation was…. I was a Middle Manager NOT a Middle Leader. To move forward, I needed to consider what I was actually doing with and for the learning of the teachers and students in my school.
> (Middle Leader, Peita Lack, 2018)

This is not to say that middle leading does not involve management per se, but rather to highlight that we focus specifically on professional learning, and any management would be directly related to facilitating such professional learning.

Table 1.1 Examples of middle leading roles and not middle leading roles

Middle leading roles	Not middle leading roles
• Senior teacher • Head of department • Level coordinator • Instructional leader • Process leader • Development leader • Curriculum coordinator	• Principal • Systemic curriculum advisor • School manager • Vice principal

What is middle leading for?

A critical question for the middle leader is – what is middle leading for? Middle leading is an educational practice (in a broad sense); and like other educational practices it is part of the complex of education practices aiming for the formation and transformation of individuals and societies (this is described more fully in the next chapter). This broad purpose of education aims to support others (individuals and collectives) *to live well in a world worth living in* (Kemmis and Edwards-Groves, 2018). As Keith Basso reminds us (1996) in his work with Apache peoples, each one of us offers a different take on the significance of place for our lives and for our learning, for living well in a world worth living in. Conceptions of wisdom, manners, and morals, and of our own histories, experiences, and knowledges are inextricably intertwined with place – our own place, our 'sense of place'. A central purpose for leading is to recognise and respond to the place, and to each individual teacher's histories, experiences, and knowledges.

In education practice, therefore, middle leading primarily seeks to support place focused learning and development in schools – of teachers and of students. This is about learning and teaching to live well in a world worth living in through practices that form, *reform*, and *transform*. The middle leader does this by initiating teachers and students into thinking critically about: i) their histories, experiences, and knowledges; ii) their language, their actions, and their relationships; iii) what they are doing as they engage in new or developing activities; and iv) how they relate to others in ways that promote agency and solidarity. To do this, middle leaders must begin by asking of themselves particular kinds of searching questions; for instance:

1. Does the educational activity initiate *teachers and students* into forms of understanding that foster individual and collective self-expression: the capacity to understand our world, and to think and speak well? Does it model and help to secure a culture based on reason in the classroom, the school, and the community beyond?
2. Does the educational activity initiate *teachers and students* into modes of action that foster individual and collective self-development: the capacities to do the things we need to survive and thrive as biological beings and as people and communities, and to act well in the material and natural world, and in the economic life of the local and global communities? Does it model and help to secure a productive economy and a sustainable world in the classroom, the school, and the community beyond?
3. Does the educational activity initiate *teachers and students* into ways of relating to others and to the world that foster individual and collective self-determination, that is, democratic self-determination: the capacities to relate well to others and the world as social and political beings committed to democracy, justice, care, and compassion, for example? Does it model and help to secure a just and democratic society in the classroom, the school, and the community beyond?

(Kemmis and Edwards-Groves, 2018, p. 24)

For the middle leader, these kinds of broad theoretical questions solidify the base from which to act in purposeful ways in practices in places. These are questions that frame what can be asked of any educational formation or any educational innovation; and form a strong foundation that provides insight into the purposes of educational work. They are questions that challenge us all to reconnect with past practices as a platform to grow and change. As Kemmis and Edwards-Groves (2018) suggest, they are questions that:

> open windows into education—to see how ways of doing education were formed and developed, and how they evolved and transformed over time, sometimes disappearing altogether. They also open windows out from education, to see how educational formations and innovations served or did not serve the interests of the cultures, economies and societies they intended to serve. They help to answer the question 'To what extent does education mirror and to what extent does it shape societies?' (It always does some of both.)
>
> (p. vii)

This proposition is one that is not only important, but central for middle leading. It places at the centre of thought and action the need to consider both the broad purpose of education and its impact on individuals and societies, and the local happeningness of it as it is developed in schools and classrooms. Middle leading is part of the indivisible connection between practices and places. Leading education into successful futures is leveraged from a deep knowledge and strong sense of the current and past practices (in and of that place); for the middle leader, its purpose to facilitate teacher learning for student learning connects directly to these site-based knowledges and practices.

Middle leading

Now we have clarified who middle leaders are and the purpose of middle leading, we want to direct attention to outlining and discussing the practice of middle leading – what it is comprised of and how it can be understood. This is important because, as noted above, it is not the same as the leading of principals, and so we need new conceptual tools to explore this domain of educational leading.

After working with a range of middle leaders across different countries (Australia, Canada, New Zealand, Sweden) at different levels (early childhood, primary, secondary, tertiary), we have distilled some of the key practices of middle leaders. These are presented as simultaneously practiced couplings: *leading and teaching; managing and facilitating;* and *collaborating and communicating*.

6 *Leading from the middle*

> **The practice of middle leading** involves engaging in (simultaneous) *leading and teaching* by *managing and facilitating* educational development through *collaborating and communicating* to create communicative spaces for sustainable future action.
>
> (Grootenboer, Rönnerman and Edwards-Groves, 2017, p. 248)

The key idea here is that middle leaders are always (or often) simultaneously engaging in leading and teaching, and that these two practices are interrelated; they are always (or often) simultaneously engaging in managing and facilitating professional learning, and that these two practices are interrelated; and they are always (or often) simultaneously engaging in collaborating and communicating, and that these two practices are interrelated.

> Taking these broader practices together, middle leading is a deliberate educative practice that seeks to *build* individual and collective capacity and school-based coherence of site-based education development from, within, and beyond the middle, as its practices effectively and strategically extend in dialogic ways upward to the principal and executive leadership, and down and across to teachers in classrooms in pursuit of learning, development, and change.

The *leading and teaching* coupling highlights that middle leaders are both leading pedagogical and curriculum development in their particular site (e.g. department or group), and engaging in the same pedagogical and curriculum development in their own teaching. They cannot simply offer a course or workshop on a particular idea or approach 'from a distance', nor can they concern themselves only with their own classroom – they must be intimately involved in both, and in an integrated way. This may well involve being an outstanding teacher themselves, opening up their teaching practices to others (e.g. through allowing other teachers to engage with and/or observe classroom practice), and visiting the classrooms of colleagues. A desired emphasis in teacher professional learning relates to the power of self-regulation as practitioners assume personal and professional responsibility that leads them to see themselves as agents for the kind of change that will contribute to improvement in learning outcomes for their students. Such a focus of attention upon teachers themselves cannot be denied; however, we suggest it is the middle leader role that lies at the centre of augmenting successful and sustainable professional learning in among teachers in schools. It is a practice that traverses *leading and teaching* in schools.

The *managing and facilitating* coupling is an important dimension of middle leading practice primarily because it relates to creating and facilitating spaces and the enabling conditions for pedagogical and curriculum development. Of course, there is a 'mountain of administration' that needs to be undertaken for schools to run effectively, and middle leaders will no doubt be charged with undertaking some of this work as they develop and facilitate the professional learning. Part of the work for some middle leaders, is to participate in their school's executive leadership team, but they (the executive leader and the middle leader them self) need to guard against administrative duties becoming overwhelming, overriding, and all-consuming. So, middle leading does involve managing and facilitating but not primarily as 'busy administrative work' imposing more bureaucratic tasks distributed from the principal and senior leadership. Primarily, it has to be about making a difference in the pedagogy and learning in the classroom. Indeed, the only reason all the layers of bureaucracy and management exist is because teachers and students meet in classrooms to learn. Thus, managing and facilitating by middle leaders is fundamentally different from the administrative work undertaken by principals. This is because middle leading is specifically focused on classroom teaching and learning practices. To illustrate, a common activity that all middle leaders engage in, is meeting and assembling staff in a range of 'meeting' arrangements. However, this is not like a whole school staff meeting which have a hierarchical nature and where the focus might be on the administration and management of school routines. Rather, middle leaders may organise group meetings with teaching colleagues or teams to explore and develop pedagogy and curriculum, and these would be more collegial and interactive. These sorts of staff meetings still require management (through organisation, preparation and orchestration) and facilitation (through skilfully scaffolding the teacher learning as the meeting itself is happening) on the behalf of the middle leader. This is an example of the dimension of simultaneously *managing and facilitating* to which we refer.

Third, middle leaders engage in *collaborating and communicating* as fundamental middle leading practices. Indeed, it is clear from the preceding two 'couplings' that effective collaboration and communication is required. Essentially, it is crucial that middle leaders work collaboratively with their teaching peers because they are reliant on them to achieve the goals and purposes of their leading work – good learning and teaching across all classrooms. Middle leaders cannot do this alone. Additionally, it is not enough to only ensure that good teaching and learning occurs in their own classroom. This condition can be quite complex for middle leaders who are often appointed based on their 'good teaching', yet now they are charged with developing the learning and teaching across a range of classrooms. This means their influence is provisional, since, in reality, it is also mediated by the practices of other teachers. Collaborating and communicating with and among teaching teams becomes imperative to their work. Added to this, middle leaders need to work with the senior leadership to ensure their leading is comprehensible to, and consistent with, the directions and purposes of the whole school strategic development agenda. This is a relational endeavour, an aspect of middle leading we will deal with in a later section; but needless to say, is that *collaboration and communication* are central and

8 *Leading from the middle*

necessary features of (and conditions for) the leading, teaching, managing, and facilitating practices that enable site-based education and its development.

Obviously, as is clear from the description of the three couplings, these dimensions of middle leading are not independent from each other, and although we have presented and discussed them separately, they are always realised in practice an integrated, simultaneously enacted fashion. Below is a brief example, a *story from practice*, to illustrate the interdependency of these dimensions as they are experienced by middle leader, Davis.

> Davis was the Dean of Year 7 (students aged 12–13 years) in his primary school and this meant that he had oversight of the pastoral care of the Year 7 students. There were five classes in Year 7 with six core teachers (including Davis). There had been some concern about bullying in the school, and so the school decided to address this, and Davis was to lead this initiative in his middle leading role as Year 7 Dean. To this end, he organised their next Year level meeting to focus on this issue, and he facilitated a collegial discussion on bullying in the school, and the ways it could be addressed in the classroom. The group then committed to developing some classroom resources, and to collectively monitor their impact on student learning and behaviour. Davis then managed the preparation and sharing of the resources, facilitated the opportunities for staff to observe the corresponding lessons in the classroom, created a plan for an 'endorsed' teacher time to watch the students in the playground, and supported teachers in some ways to collect some evidence about the issue. Davis himself also taught with the resources and both observed in his colleagues' classrooms and had some of them observe in his. After four weeks, Davis organised a second staff meeting for the group to individually and collectively reflect on and review the evidence they had collected, accounting for the feelings and views of all the teachers involved; after this meeting, as a group they decided to engage in a second round of information gathering with a focus on understanding more about the perpetrators, victims, and bystanders.

Despite the lack of detail, in this quite simple 'everyday' example, you can see that Davis was engaged in leading and teaching, managing and facilitating, and collaborating and communicating, but with the purpose of provisioning authentic student learning (in this case teachers with students understanding and addressing bullying). As noted previously, these three tenets are ideas that will be picked up throughout the book.

Understanding middle leading: positioning, practice, and praxis

There may be many ways to understand middle leading, but as we have made clear, we see middle leading being fundamentally about professional learning as it happens in schools. Previously we have conceptualised middle leading (Grootenboer, Edwards-Groves and Rönnerman, 2014; Grootenboer, Rönnerman and Edwards-Groves, 2017) as having four characteristics or facets:

1. *Positional* – middle leaders are positioned and relationally structured 'between' the senior leadership and the teachers. This means that they are functioning members of both groups.
2. *Philosophical* – middle leading practices are in the centre of the action – alongside their colleagues.
3. *Practical* – here we are concerned with the actual practical work of middle leading – what middle leaders say, do, and feel, and how they relate and build connections.
4. *Praxeological* – that is, middle leading is a form of praxis where their practices come from a moral and ethical commitment to their community of learners.

Positional: middle leaders undertake their practices *between* the principal's leadership and the pedagogical practices of classroom teachers. In this way, it can be seen that middle leaders have to relate *upwards* to the principal, and *down and across* to their teaching colleagues (see Figure 1.1).

This diagram illustrates how we consider the positional place for middle leading: that middle leaders are not so much in a special group of their own, but rather their practices are associated both with the formal leadership of the school, and the classroom teachers, and that they are an integral part of both groups. Their work is constituted by leading from, within, and beyond the

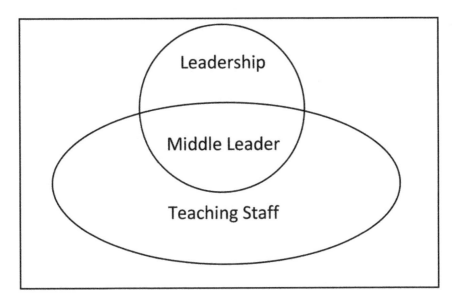

Figure 1.1 Positioning of the middle leader

middle. Thus, the middle leader works from, within, and beyond the complexities of a sort of relational and structural sandwich (Grootenboer, Edwards-Groves and Rönnerman, 2014), and this can be an awkward space at times. Clearly there are many relational issues that can emerge for a middle leader given their positioning, and the breakdown of relationships with the senior leadership and/or some of their teaching team can be damaging and difficult. It is crucial, then, that they can build and maintain strong professional collegial relationships in their school sites. A key facet of this is relational trust; this concept will be discussed briefly later in this chapter, and then in a more focused way later in the book. However, it is also the case that middle leaders have the most significant influence on the professional learning and development of their teaching peers and colleagues (Edwards-Groves and Rönnerman, 2012), as opposed to the principal who can be seen as too distant from the classroom (Lingard, Hayes, Mills and Christie, 2003) to actually have direct impact on the learning of students. Thus, the positioning of middle leaders provides a unique opportunity to impact the core business of schooling – learning.

Philosophical: To use a sporting metaphor, a middle leader might be considered like the captain of the team, who still must play the game, rather than the coach, who leads from the sidelines. They are in the action and everyday practices of the classroom, doing the grounded work of education in practical ways. They are not some heroic crusader who has come to single-handedly rescue the teaching team, nor do they have all the answers. Of course, there is an inherent difficulty here for middle leaders because their credibility as a leader will be determined, at least partially, by their capacity to maintain good teaching practice themselves, and to do this while also having a vested interest in the teaching practices of their colleagues. Nevertheless, middle leading can bring about real and sustainable educational development in school sites because they can empathise and understand the context of teaching in the school, and have some capacity to lead change and growth.

Practical: We are aware that there is quite a body of literature that talks about the qualities, traits, and characteristics of 'good' leaders. We are not so concerned about such things, because we see that there is scope for a wide range of people to be leaders, each with their own strengths and qualities, and all with the capacity to develop. With this in mind, our focus is on the practices of middle leading – how middle leading unfolds in real school sites. This can have a range of implications, but perhaps most prominent is the understanding that middle leading is a site-based practice. In other words, it is practiced and developed in response to the particular conditions and arrangements in a school, including the needs of the learners and the community. So 'good' middle leading practice will look different in each site, and we do not seek to identify or describe any sort of 'middle leading *best practice*', as fundamentally we do not think that such a thing exists. Rather we would talk about a 'promising responsive practice', one that throws a wider net over realistic possibilities for practice that is responsive to sites and circumstances and orients the thinking of practitioners to a future based on hope, growth, and reasonable progressions forward. For example, would the middle leading practices of the Head of a Science faculty in a large secondary school be the same as the practices of a syndicate leader in a small primary school? We do not think so, and so throughout this book we will endeavour to provoke and support middle leaders to develop their own middle leading practices in response to the specific needs and conditions of their site.

Praxeological (as praxis): This is perhaps a new word for many, but to us it simply highlights the practical wisdom of middle leading, and a responsiveness to the critical needs of the school site. In particular, it means that middle leading is an ethical and moral practice with ramifications and implications for the students and the school community. Also, it is about acting or doing something, not just discussing issues and concerns philosophically or theoretically, but actually doing something responsively, this is in response to the particular and unique needs of the school site. This is called *praxis*, and 'praxis is what people do when they take into account all the circumstances and exigencies that confront them at a particular moment and then, taking the broadest view they can of what is best to do, they act' (Kemmis and Smith, 2008, p. 4). Of course, middle leaders are working with principals, teachers, and students, and often in complex demographic and/or social-political situations, and so there are always ethical considerations needing to be made, particularly when in education the outcomes of practices cannot really be known until afterwards. Underpinning this position lies an ethical commitment by the middle leader to support others in socially just and morally informed ways. Nevertheless, in these complex relational and positional situations, middle leaders must act, and so it is important that these dimensions need to be foregrounded in understandings of their practices.

To illustrate these four dimensions as they are experienced in the day-to-day realities of middle leading, we offer the following short *story from practice*:

> Katarina was the numeracy coordinator in her middle school; she worked two days a week across all the classes to improve the numeracy pedagogy of the teachers, and the skills and knowledge of the students. She was 'on class' the other three days. While she was committed to improving the broader numeracy skills, knowledge, and attitudes of the students, many of whom seemed to dislike mathematics, she was well aware that her principal was most concerned about the school's results in the national numeracy test (NAPLAN, where the results of which were published annually and often used to compare schools). Thus, while the aims of Katarina and the principal were not diametrically opposed, there was some tension. In particular, there was some pressure from the principal to 'prepare the students for the test', but some of the staff felt that 'teaching to the test' was making the students dislike numeracy even more. In her own class, Katarina felt this tension between preparing the students for the national test so that the pressure of

> the test-taking was reduced for them, but at the same time she had a bigger picture aim to develop healthy mathematical attitudes among her students. Leading and teaching for Katarina, thus created in-practice tensions. Nevertheless, she had to act as both a leader and a teacher. To this end she selected some of the test items, and developed them into some more pedagogically robust activities that related well to the learners in her school. She shared these with her teaching colleagues, and as a result of this action teachers, with her guidance, subsequently went on to collaboratively create some more resources that were designed to be based on good teaching practices and at the same time prepare the students to more confidently sit the national test.

For the sake of space, a lot of the detail is not included here, but Katarina's story shows how she had to conduct her practice:

- from a position between the teaching staff and the principal;
- beyond the classroom to meet the principal's key improvement agenda;
- as one also in the thick of her own teaching milieu;
- in practical ways that were responsive to the various needs of the site; and
- to act in ways that were morally and ethically defensible vis-à-vis the students' needs.

Generative leadership and trust

In 2012 Edwards-Groves and Rönnerman discussed the idea of 'generative leadership', which focuses specifically on leading professional learning through action research. Essentially, this involves the leading of learning – leading the professional development of teachers as learners (about teaching) so they can then facilitate student learning in their own classrooms. This leading is regularly undertaken by middle leaders, and is based on reciprocity between professional learning practices and leading practices. They commented:

> From this perspective, learning and leading practices take form in, and are formed by living the practice in 'the site of the social'. In our view, this mutual accomplishment is necessary for generating learning and leading capacities.
>
> (p. 17)

Thus, educational middle leading can be seen as generative when the leading and professional learning are contemplated simultaneously. In other words, middle leading can be considered as *generative* when it is based on sustained and focused professional learning in response to local needs and conditions. That said, these arrangements and conditions to support this sort of leading are not necessarily always found in educational sites, and so this requires some intentionality and strategic structuring to allow middle leaders to focus on facilitating professional learning. We suggest that action research is one effective way to do this, and we talk more about this in Chapter 3.

A foundational requirement for this form of leading is trust, and we will discuss this more extensively later (in Chapter 4), but because of its centrality for creating enabling conditions for professional learning we briefly discuss it here. Trust seems to be a factor mentioned extensively in relation to effective leading in educational sites, and without it, reform and development efforts collapse rather quickly. It also appears that trust is something that takes a while to build and develop, but it can be rapidly destroyed and lost through one thoughtless comment or act. In short – trust is a precious commodity for leaders and needs to be nurtured and reassured. This sort of trust is multidimensional, and involves inter-personal relationships, interactions between colleagues, confidence and dependability, and pragmatic empathy and understanding. We see trust as the 'glue' that can hold a community together, and therefore, it needs to be a central concern for educational leaders, including middle leaders.

Themes and the organisation of the book

This book is fundamentally a book for middle leaders. Although it is based on a long history of empirical research with teachers and middle leaders across Sweden, Australia, Canada, and New Zealand, it is not a research book per se. Rather, we are looking to present and discuss some of the important features we have discovered about middle leading, and how they relate to the practice of middle leading in educational sites – it is about theory *in practice*.

While there appears to be a wide variety and range of training and professional development for principals, middle leaders seem to be somewhat neglected in terms of support and preparation for their leading work – this book seeks to address that gap. For this reason, we have included reflective discussion questions at the end of each chapter, along with some further recommended reading. To provide purchase upon how 'new information' can be integrated into existing repertoires of practice we use *stories from practice* as exemplifications that allow for a grounded interpretation of the aspect of practice being discussed in each chapter. We note, each of these have been drawn from our own research and been subject to external interrogation and critique. We imagine that this would be useful for a group of middle leaders to work through collaboratively through shared reading and dialogue, and it may even lead to a communicative space that supports on-going action research into middle leading practices.

The book is divided into seven chapters.

1   *Leading from the middle*
2   *Practices and practice architectures of middle leading*
3   *School-based professional learning and development*
4   *Relating, trust, and dialogic practice in middle leading*

5   Evidence-informed development
6   Middle leading in practice: criticality and impact in schools
7   Middle leading as a practice-changing practice

In Chapter 2: *Practices and practice architectures of middle leading*, we provide a conceptual framework to understand middle leading and the conditions that shape it in practice. Practice is a term that is widely used, but not necessarily clearly understood, and so in this chapter we outline a *theory of practice* – specifically the 'theory of practice architectures' (Kemmis, Wilkinson, Edwards-Groves, Hardy, Grootenboer and Bristol, 2014). However, it is important to note that this is not just an abstract or esoteric discussion, but rather it is about how we can understand practices (in this case middle leading practices) as they unfold in real sites (like schools). Furthermore, the theory of 'ecologies of practices' (Kemmis *et al.*, 2014) is also outlined to explain and understand how practices relate to one another, like how teaching practices are intimately connected to students' learning practices. Together, these theoretical tools show how middle leading practices are fundamentally *site-based*, and need to be understood, developed, and practised in real school sites. Furthermore, it shows that it is nonsensical at anything other than the most broad and general level, to talk about *best practice* as if it can be relevant to different schools, departments, groups, and contexts – in essence, practices are made and remade in every site as a *promising practice*. This understanding of middle leading as practice will equip the middle leader to lead and facilitate change and development in their school.

Chapter 3: *School-based professional learning and development*, contains a practical, philosophical, and theoretical outline of action research as the vehicle to drive and sustain professional learning in school sites. As was clear in this chapter, we see the fundamental role of the middle leaders as leading professional learning – pedagogical and curriculum development, and we are convinced that action research is the best way to structure, organise, and sustain this growth. Furthermore, action research is collaborative and evidence-based, thus providing the means for developing a *community of practice* amongst the teachers in the team, department, or group, and ensuring that development is robust and responsive to the needs of the school community (i.e. fundamentally the students). In this chapter we provide practical ideas for middle leaders to develop action research in their schools, including ways to develop and sustain a *communicative space*, and solid and practical ways to collect and analyse data. This sort of research is not about developing a generalised theory or universal answer to a big problem – it is about practitioner enquiry into their own practices in their own sites. Kemmis *et al.* (2014) said, in teacher action research 'we do not aim to produce generalisations about the "one best way" to do things. In fact, we don't want to find the best way to do things anywhere *except* here – where we are, in our situation' (p. 69).

Chapter 4: *Relating, trust, and dialogic practice in middle leading*, centres on the relational nature of middle leading, and has a strong focus on matters of *trust*. It is widely known that trust is vital for strong school leadership and educational development, and so here we outline what it involves and ways it can be sustained and developed. Specifically, a discussion is provided of the five dimensions of trust that are pertinent for school middle leadership: (1) interpersonal trust; (2) interactional trust; (3) intersubjective trust; (4) intellectual trust; and (5) pragmatic trust. Practical examples are used to show how these five dimensions have been nurtured by middle leaders' dialogic practices. We show how creating a relational space through dialogue makes trust possible. The reciprocity between relational trust and dialogic approaches to professional learning are explored in this chapter. Through building and sustaining trust, a vibrant professional community can be established that can sustain ongoing professional learning and curriculum development in response to local needs and conditions.

Chapter 5: *Evidence-informed development*, provides specific comment on the increasing demand for schools and school leaders to collect and work with 'data' vis-à-vis student and school performance. In particular, this has become a large part of middle leaders' roles, and while it adds to their workloads, it does not necessarily seem to lead to improved learning and teaching practices or outcomes. In this chapter we try and shift the discourse from one about 'data' to a more helpful one on 'evidence'. Specifically, in this chapter some practical methods and tools to collect and analyse evidence will be outlined and exemplified, so a middle leader can think about ways to meaningfully and manageably use evidence to inform development in response to the needs of the students and teachers involved.

Chapter 6: *Criticality and impact in middle leading: stories from the field*, is a chapter that contains four *stories from practice* of middle leading in action, which are drawn from actual middle leading we have observed and analysed in our research. These short *stories from practice* are vignettes of practice designed to practically illustrate some of the key points that have been made in earlier chapters. They are not presented as recipes to follow or necessarily examples of outstanding practice – indeed some show frustration, tension, and problems. Rather, they show the criticality required for impact in the experiences of some middle leaders as they seek to lead professional learning in their particular sites. Each story is briefly discussed as presented; we hope that each case will cause the reader to stop and pause to reflect critically on their own middle leading practices. From these stories, we generate a few common issues that seem to arise across cases, and these are also briefly discussed at the end of the chapter. These include the perennial concern related to time (or lack thereof), the use and analysis of evidence, and maintaining a critical stance.

Finally, in Chapter 7, *Middle leading as a practice-changing practice*, we return to some of the key themes of the book to prompt reflection and thought about your middle leading. As was made clear earlier, this book is not just a book of information or ideas for your interest – it is meant to equip and provoke you to develop your own middle leading practices, in your own site, with your own professional community, and in response to the needs of your own student community. Specifically, we look at how middle leading can be understood as *action-oriented professional learning*. We conclude this final chapter by taking a 'realistic' look at how the 'messiness' of school life can sometimes confound middle leaders' efforts to realise educational reform.

An extensive set of resources, templates and tools are also provided in the Appendix at the conclusion of the book. These can be used and modified to suit the particular needs and context of the middle leader's professional learning and curriculum development.

Theory-into-practice (TIPs): questions for reflection and discussion

1. In this chapter we have claimed that middle leaders are the key agents in leading professional learning – curriculum and pedagogical development. In what ways does this reflect your current role?
2. Earlier we suggested that middle leaders work in some sort of 'relational and structural sandwich', and that this can be difficult for many. As a middle leader, how do you experience simultaneously being a formal leader and a classroom teacher? What are the tensions and affordances of this relational positioning?
3. Can you do an 'audit' of your *managing and facilitating* practices. How much of it is related to the school management, organisation, and systems? How much is directly related to teaching and learning in your department or group?
4. Middle leading is a form of *praxis*. How do you understand the moral and ethical dimension of your practices? How do you determine the best course of action when the path ahead is not clear?
5. Discuss the centrality of trust to your middle leading practices. How do you develop and sustain trust? What diminishes it?

References

Basso, K. (1996). *Wisdom Sits in Places: Landscape and Language Among the Western Apache*. Albuquerque, New Mexico, US: University of New Mexico Press.
Edwards Groves, C. and Rönnerman, K. (2012). 'Generating leading practices through professional learning', *Professional Development in Education*, 39(1), 122–140.
Edwards-Groves, C., Grootenboer, P. and Rönnerman, K. (2016). 'Facilitating a culture of relational trust in school-based action research: recognising the role of middle leaders', *Educational Action Research*, 24(3), 369–386.
Fullan, M. (2015). *The New Meaning of Educational Change*, 5th edition. New York: Teachers' College Press.
Grootenboer, P., Edwards-Groves and Rönnerman, K. (2014). 'Leading practice development: Voices from the middle', *Professional Development in Education*, 41(3), 508–526.
Grootenboer, P., Rönnerman, K. and Edwards-Groves, C. (2017). Leading from the Middle: A Praxis-Oriented Practice. In P. Grootenboer, C. Edwards-Groves, and S.

Choy (Eds), *Practice Theory Perspectives on Pedagogy and Education: Praxis, diversity and contestation* (pp. 243–263). Singapore: Springer.
Hargreaves, A. and Ainscow, M. (2015). 'The top and bottom of leadership and change', *Phi Delta Kappan*, 97(3), 42–48.
Kemmis, S. and Smith, T. (2008). Praxis and praxis development. In S. Kemmis and T. Smith (Eds), *Enabling praxis: Challenges for education* (pp. 3–15). Amsterdam: Sense.
Kemmis, S. and Edwards-Groves, C. (2018). *Understanding Education: History, Politics and Practices*. Singapore: Springer.
Kemmis, S., Wilkinson, J., Edwards-Groves, C., Hardy, I., Grootenboer, P. and Bristol, L. (2014). *Changing Practices, Changing Education*. Singapore: Springer.
Lingard, B., Hayes, D., Mills, M. and Christie, P. (2003). *Leading learning: Making hope practical in schools*. Maidenhead, UK: Open University Press.

Further reading

Grootenboer, P. (2018). *The practices of school middle leadership: Leading professional learning*. Singapore: Springer.
Ministry of Education. (2012). *Leading from the Middle: educational leadership for middle and senior leaders*. Wellington, NZ: Learning Media.

2 Practices and practice architectures of middle leading

Changing practices in schools, and supporting others to do so, first requires understanding the particular factors that both influence and successfully enable the change process to move forward in the school. For middle leaders, this means coming to an understanding about four things:

1 How middle leading is connected to other education practices in the school;
2 The intellectual, practical, and relational spaces necessary for pedagogical leadership, and how to create such spaces for leading;
3 The factors, or as we prefer to say, the conditions or practice architectures, that support and challenge middle leading practices; and
4 Developing a *theory-of-practice-for-action*.

In this chapter, we provide a conceptual framework to understand middle leading and the conditions that shape it *in practice*. This conceptual framework is important since the term 'practice' has become so overused that it has now not as clearly understood as it could be. Practice – being a commonly used term in the field of education – is generally used to refer broadly to something that is *being done*. We want to clarify this point further in this chapter.

To address this lack of clarity, in this chapter we come to a *theory of practice* – specifically *the theory of practice architectures* (Kemmis et al., 2014). This theory provides a useful frame of reference for understanding practices (in this case middle leading practices) as they happen in places where education happens (like in staffrooms or classrooms in schools). Ultimately, it provides you as middle leaders with a useful way to understand, frame, and develop your leading practices as you work to support school-based development, professional learning, and change. We position middle leading *as* pedagogical leadership, and as necessary for supporting practice development in schools that primarily functions to improve student learning (its outcomes and its practices).

Middle leading as connected to other education practices

The work of the middle leader touches all dimensions of education in schools. It is generally connected up with, and intricately entangled with other education practices concerned with:

- teaching
- student learning
- professional learning
- leading and administration and
- researching and evaluation.

From the first chapter, we know that one important but driving feature of the work of the middle leader is *teaching*. As a teacher, the middle leader essentially continues to focus on the development of effective pedagogies for supporting students in their learning in his/her own classroom. Thus, *student learning* forms a core, and fundamental concern for the middle leader. Emerging from this is his/her more widely recognised level of expertise, experience, competence and commitment towards teaching and learning in the school; and so, the middle leader (as a teacher-leader and leading teacher) is often given the responsibility for leading the *professional learning* of colleagues. Moreover, because of a genuine commitment for designing quality teaching for student learning, coupled with an interest in supporting other teachers do the same (through professional learning), in many instances it is the middle leader who works closely with or is part of the school leadership team. Participating in *leading* and designing school-based professional learning projects, activities or programmes (including supporting the conduct of action research), the middle leader's work with the principal, the executive leadership team or with other middle leaders, form part of a broader pedagogical, policy, curriculum, or overall reform agenda in schools. Their leading practices are often directed by *researching and evaluating* that shapes the national or state education agendas or policies (e.g. national curriculums, testing regimes, or professional standards), and sometimes extend, in practical terms, beyond the school to work with teachers in other schools in the municipality, school district or other regional jurisdictions. We also know that:

> The middle leader is a pedagogical leader in the school. Hence, middle leading *is* pedagogical leadership because its practices relate to student learning in classrooms, pedagogical practice and teaching, professional learning and development, leading and leadership, and researching and evaluating outcomes.

What we can see here is that the work of the middle leader is not uni-dimensional, it is in fact part of a multifaceted, overlapping complex of other

20 *Practices and practice architectures*

practices connected to education. These connected education practices form what has been described by Kemmis and colleagues (2014) as part of the *Education Complex of Practices* (see Figure 2.1 below).

A close look at this diagram raises three matters for consideration for the middle leader:

- First, and most simply, that it could be said that all education practices are connected to one another in an ecology of practices;
- Second, that like an ecology (in a biological sense), education practices exist in dynamic interdependent relationships with one another; and
- Third, practices like learning and teaching require suitable conditions that are receptive to change, adaptation, and development (like an ecological niche).

Each of these education practices directly and indirectly connect to the other in varying, asymmetrical, and diverse ways; and so rarely do they exist uniformly, harmoniously, or seamlessly without some degree of tension, pressure, resistance or struggle. This has important implications for the language, work, and power of the middle leader. We consider this in more detail next.

For the middle leader, the idea of aligning their work within an *ecology of practices* perspective (Grootenboer, 2018) raises these key questions:

- *Where does middle leading fit?*
- *What enables and constrains middle leading?*

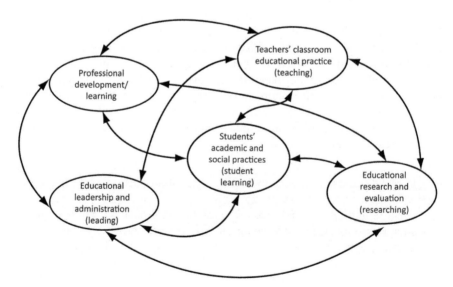

Figure 2.1 The education complex of practices
(Kemmis et al., 2014)

Practices and practice architectures 21

The reality is, middle leading is a practice that *more directly* influences each of the other education practices of the school. Our research shows this – hence we represent middle leading more like as shown in Figure 2.2 below.

This representation depicts how we see the practice of middle leading – as central to all education practices in a school's formation and transformation. We say that *middle leading is a practice-changing practice*. Furthermore, it connects up or hangs together more intimately with *all* education practices in the complex; that is, with:

- *Student learning practices*, whereby your ongoing regular day-to-day work, is first and foremost that of being a teacher focused on teaching students in classrooms by supporting their learning outcomes and learning practices as individuals and a cohort.

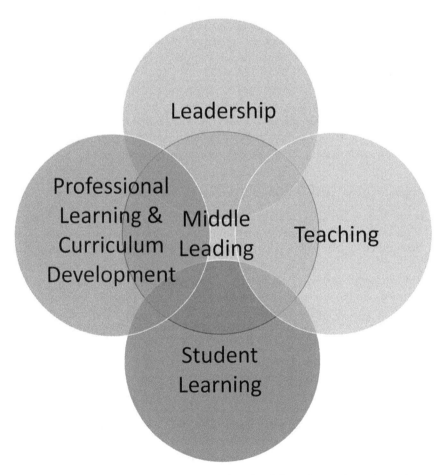

Figure 2.2 The centrality of middle leading for school formation and transformation

- *Teaching practices*, whereby they are primarily and routinely focused on how particular teaching and pedagogical practices (from planning, implementing, assessing, evaluating, reporting, developing) support students' learning and development both in the immediate short-term teaching of a lesson and in the longer-term programming and curriculum development.
- *Professional learning practices*, whereby middle leaders are largely responsible for leading professional learning and development in the school, by managing and facilitating educational development through collaborating and communicating with your colleagues and with the school leadership team.
- *Leading practices*, whereby as part of the school leadership team the middle leader shares in the responsibility for contributing to the design and decision making related to curriculum development in the school and underpinned by varying discipline-related policy initiatives.
- *Researching and evaluation practices*, since the middle leader responsible for curriculum in the school, they seek out current research related to their discipline, learn about, participate in and often facilitate the implementation of action research among colleagues, lead the evaluation of student results in the discipline or school, and so on.

Therefore, knowing that professional work is intricately connected to, and highly contingent on, other educational work in the school is helpful for understanding and developing middle leading practices. It also alerts those who support middle leaders (the principal, the other executive staff, or the district office personnel for example) come to grips with the complexity of the work middle leaders do.

Middle leading within the education complex of practices

If, as we suggest, middle leading is situated within a complex of other education practices, then it stands to reason that it is influenced (both supported and challenged) by these other practices. This means middle leading is mediated, shaped, or influenced by the very particular needs of other individuals with whom you (as the middle leader) work with (students, colleagues, principals, other executive staff) and specific circumstances in the places (or sites) in which the practice of middle leading occurs (the demographic, geographic social-political, and social-economic conditions of the school community). But it is also not that simple: each of these other education practices are variously influenced by middle leading. Thus, middle leading both mediates and is mediated; shapes and is shaped; or influences and is influenced. Accordingly, middle leading is a dynamic practice that both impacts and is impacted upon by site-based conditions AND, as we know, these conditions will be different between middle leaders and the schools in which they work. We describe these mediating dimensions of practice as *practice architectures* or the shaping machinery of practices – this will be discussed more fully in a later section of the chapter. Knowing that your practices are never neutral is essential for understanding, accounting for and responding to possible contingencies and exigencies that may affect your work.

We now turn to a *story from practice*, presented as a case study, to help illustrate middle leading within the Education Complex of Practices. To help bridge the gulf between a simpler view and a richer, more complex way of understanding the concept of practice we will present an example from middle leading in a primary school. This example (extended story from practice) can be drawn on to provide empirical or practical illustrations of the theoretical and conceptual points being made in this chapter. It also helps you locate meanings about what your middle leading practice is *in* practice.

Orchestrating middle leading: a case study of middle leading at Bushland Primary School

Bushland Primary School is a small-medium rural school located in a regional school district in inland NSW, Australia. Its classes draw students from the local village and surrounding farming area. For a number of years, this school, like others in the district had been developing and implementing policies that encourage the use of a range of technologies and digital literacies to improve classroom teaching and student learning (in all curriculum areas). The broader district policy directions influenced the particular education practices related to student learning, teaching, professional development, leading, and researching in the school. At Bushland Primary School, Alena was the Year 5 teacher, the assistant principal (with a half-day release from face-to-face teaching to conduct a number of evaluation and administration tasks) and the person given the responsibility for supporting the other teachers develop their familiarity, competency, and flexibility with using digital technologies in their pedagogical practice. We note that sometimes this responsibility shifted to other teachers on the staff depending on the nature of the discipline. Specifically, for the teachers at Bushland Primary School, Alena was responsible for supporting the effective use of smartboards and iPads for instruction.

At Bushland Primary School the principal was very supportive of this professional development initiative and thereby provided Alena with additional time to prepare the project and the material for the after school professional learning sessions and to visit the other teachers in their classrooms in a coaching/mentoring role. It was Alena's responsibility for this overall project of professional learning. As a middle leader, she facilitated focused meetings so that teachers could work together in teaching teams to develop their practices relating to the development of digitally-based pedagogies in their classrooms so that most students learn to use a range of digital technologies in their lessons. Alena used critical participatory action research as the main platform for guiding the roll-out of this initiative in the school. But it was not as simple as that, Alena, as primarily a classroom teacher, had the simultaneous responsibility for also developing what she describes as 'a digital turn' in her classroom lessons with her own Year 5 students.

Over the year-long project, the teachers worked together in professional learning and teaching practices associated with using the newly acquired

24 *Practices and practice architectures*

Figure 2.3 Interrelationships between 'changing' technological practices and teacher professional development

smartboard and iPads. Through conducting professional development meetings (see Figure 2.3), engaging in professional learning conversations at formal and informal meetings, hosting and participating in classroom visits and classroom 'walk-throughs', sourcing and providing additional materials and resources, being a critical friend for individual colleagues, negotiating with the principal for additional time and resources, Alena spent the year supporting her colleagues develop familiarity, knowledge, and competencies around their technology usage in lessons.

Going a little further: Although Alena had a general plan to guide the programme of activities with her colleagues, her leading practices as a teacher and a middle leader were supported and challenged (enabled and constrained) by a range of other conditions (circumstances) that existed in the school. For example:

- the district office had just released its new five-year technology plan that included school-based funding available for schools to purchase hardware;
- her colleagues were variously confident with using technology, some were frequent users and were highly competent whilst others were novices;
- some teachers had highly competent students in their class, others were more limited; some students in some classrooms knew more about using technology than their teachers;
- some teachers were very familiar with the 'language' of the digital age, others not;
- some of the classrooms had both iPads and Smartboards, whilst others only had a Smartboard;
- one teacher had a Bring-Your-Own-Device (BYOD) arrangement, others had not heard of this before; and
- sometimes the internet was reliable and sometimes the service was intermittent; some teachers knew how to 'troubleshoot' others did not.

Across the stages of the project, these conditions variously formed mitigating and extenuating influences on what activities could be done with the teachers and students. Furthermore, the teacher's levels of proficiency with the technology, with the pedagogy, with the new 'tech-speak' and with using multiple devices influenced the action research processes that Alena developed, and could develop, going forward. These site-specific circumstances enabled some things to be done and not others for the different individuals or for the group as a collective.

Connected to the broader situation in the school, Alena also had to develop her own teaching practices to teach her students to become more proficient in the practices of using multiple devices, web searching, of reading the screen differently to that of a printed page, of conducting and modifying online searches, of keying, of selecting relevant web sites, of co-producing, of negotiating, and so on. Through her own professional learning, the students in Alena's own Year 5 classroom came to both particular learning practices (procedural, or how to do this) and substantive practices (propositional, or what to know). At this school, for both Alena, the other teachers and the students in each classroom lesson, student's practices were also influenced by practices already past and other practices present at the time. In this case for example, the practice of web searching was influenced (enabled and/or constrained) by an individual student's past experiences and knowledge of it (at school and at home), the particular search engine being used, the topic the search, the familiarity with the topic, the wording of task itself, the reliability of the internet connection, the configuration of the students in groups, each teacher's own knowledge of and proficiency with the technologies, the teacher's level of involvement, the readability and reliability of the websites, and so on.

Overall, the education practices in this school were interconnected and mutually influential; continuously and simultaneously enabling and constraining, and being supported and challenged, by other practices in the school site (Kemmis *et al.*, 2014). As individuals and as a collective, teachers and students at Bushland Primary School learned to understand and speak the language of technology and digital literacies, do different activities with the resources and materials available, and relate to each other in different ways, and to artefacts (e.g. iPads, smartboards) as they began to collaborate on lesson or professional learning tasks. In this, they took up different sayings, doings and relatings. But this is too simplistic a rendering of the term practice, because in reality as illustrated in this example, practices are also influenced by other practices happening at the same time. These influential dimensions of practice are site-based conditions known as **practice architectures.**

Middle leading practices as site-based pedagogical leadership

When thinking about the specific kind of leading practices required for supporting the professional learning in a school like Bushland Primary School, middle leaders like Alena need to consider ways her practices are about teaching, coaching, mentoring, facilitating, guiding, collaborating, communicating, and other like activities. To do this leading work, a range of approaches or practices to support and suit the particular professional learning directions and requirements of colleagues are needed. For instance, middle leaders might:

- lead formal or informal professional dialogues about pedagogical change;
- lead coaching conversations among teaching teams;
- arrange inter-class visits between peers;
- conduct mentoring conversations with individuals;
- be a critical friend to individuals, teaching teams, or stage groups as they share their work (evidence of their learning);
- facilitate professional learning staff meetings;
- search out, collate, and evaluate relevant research and professional literature, resources and materials to share, distribute, and critique;
- be the trouble-shooter when others require additional support;
- guide and advise colleagues as they develop their own action research projects (for example) that aim to improve specific aspects of learning and teaching; or,
- negotiate the school professional learning plan with teachers, the principal, and/or executive staff.

This is not an exhaustive list, but rather it is indicative of the far-reaching and diverse nature of the kind of work that is the work of middle leaders. Entering into leading these kinds of professional learning practices and activities, it is important for middle leaders to think about the circumstances and conditions in their own school sites. Therefore, to respond to the situation in which they conduct their leading, middle leaders probably also consider:

- what their colleagues (and/or the students in their classrooms) already know and can do currently;
- specific activities they are going to do;
- what time and timelines will be required;
- what physical resources or materials will be needed;
- how to arrange the physical set-ups in the space available for the session/meeting;
- what specialised language or new discourses might be required to make the material accessible and understandable;
- what is going to be said and done in the session;
- how the project relates to the curriculum and the policy initiatives;
- how the project, innovation, or initiative connects to the needs of the students in the school or in the particular classes;
- how the middle leader wants to work with the group/s;
- how the teachers will work with each other as they go about their learning;
- what kinds of evidence is required to show leading and development; or,
- what is/will be the role of the principal in the project... and so on.

Taken together, these aspects of middle leading are not only interrelated but illustrate the complexity of middle leading. Leading professional learning is a project (represented in Figure 2.4 below) always made up by practices (whether specific or broad) constituted by things that are said (or sayings), work or activities being done (or doings), and people in particular kinds of relationships with one another relating to one another (teachers with other teachers, teachers and middle leaders, principals and teachers, middle leaders and principals, and so on). The idea that practices are always made up of sayings, doings, and relatings is helpful for middle leaders since these three dimensions are always ever present in the doing or accomplishing of particular education projects (like learning about digital literacies and to integrate technologies into teaching and learning).

We also know that the project of *middle leading is for site-based education development* (Kemmis et al., 2014). Site-based education development is a site-based perspective that is concerned with what happens, in reality, in real places, with real persons and critically takes account of real circumstances, experiences and conditions. And as our research has illustrated – it is a necessary condition for securing real and more sustainable change among teachers and students in schools. We also know that, in reality, middle leading is a *central cog in the machinery* of site-based education development. Understanding this feature of education practice and practice development is important for middle leaders, since as a priori, what happens and develops in one's own site is the main concern.

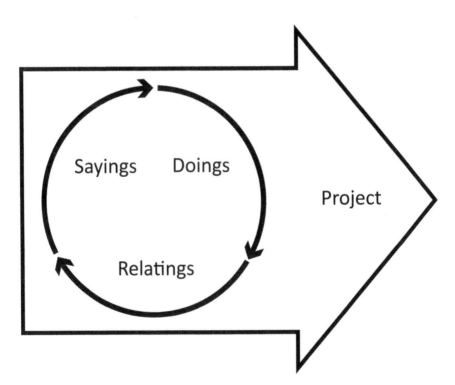

Figure 2.4 Projects as constituted by practices as constituted by sayings, doings, and relatings

> We position **middle leading practices** *as* **site-based pedagogical leadership**. We take this view since, as a priori, middle leading is for the pedagogical development of teachers for enacting high quality pedagogies with students as they learn in lessons. It is a practice-changing practice generated as site-based and site responsive.

Spaces for pedagogical leadership in the school

Supporting pedagogical change in schools requires pedagogical leadership that rests on providing the cultural, linguistic, physical and relational spaces for teacher professional learning and change. This section thus aims to support you to understand the nature of these spaces, in particular what constitutes spaces conducive for professional learning among colleagues.

A fundamental aspect of your work as a middle leader is to create supportive practices for teacher professional learning and change in your school. We use the word *create* deliberately since it connects to ideas related to doing something different to what currently exists or happens in classrooms or the school. For middle leading, this might mean innovating, fashioning, and transforming practices to generate, produce, establish, and configure changed circumstances for the teachers and the students. These broad ideals drive the practices of your work. But to generate, produce, establish, and configure practices for professional learning and change, it is necessary for middle leaders to understand the kinds of spaces (and so practices) that support and facilitate change and development.

Spaces for intersubjective meaning making

In professional learning situations teachers come together in encounters like meetings, workshops, seminars, interclass visits, or professional conversations relevant to the specific nature or purpose of the professional learning task, agenda, or goal at the time. Different kinds of tasks, agenda, goals, and purposes require specific but relevant language and discourses, different kinds of activities and resources, and different ways of working with one another. These encounters are social in nature. Therefore, as teachers encounter each other in their professional learning activities they create an *intersubjective space*. These spaces form as teachers engage in interactions and in interrelationships (Kemmis *et al.*, 2014) that provide scope for intersubjective meaning making. Intersubjective spaces evolve through particular social encounters in which shared meanings and mutual understandings between people are reached through their activities, interactions, and interrelationships in semantic space, in physical space-time and in social space.

Practices are formed in these three realms of space:

- in *semantic space* where particular *sayings* exist or develop as teachers and middle leaders use or develop a shared language so that they can create shared meanings and mutual understandings about what they are doing and what they know;
- in *physical space-time* where particular *doings* happen as teachers and middle leaders meet in shared locations in space and time to work with one another and engage in shared activities; and
- in *social space* where particular *relatings*, ways of relating and relationships exist or develop as teachers and middle leaders form different kinds of roles and collegial relationships through their shared encounters.

Thus, understanding the nature of these three realms of space and ways to 'open them up' forms an important mechanism for developing and enacting middle leading.

Opening up semantic spaces

When teachers come together for professional learning they engage in different metalanguage, discipline specific language, or professional discourses. This shared language forms a way for teachers to understand one another and/or the curriculum, programme, policy, or discipline they are learning about. Importantly this informs the sayings of the practice. Getting on the same page, so to speak, forms the *semantic space* of professional learning and necessary so that mutual understandings can be developed.

For example, at Bushland Primary School (as outlined previously) a variety of conceptualisations about technology, digital literacies, and pedagogy evolved as teachers spoke about what they were learning, what activities they were doing, and the organisational processes and procedures required to learn and practise. In the school Alena, the teachers involved in the professional learning, and the students in their lessons created a shared semantic space as they used language to arrange and describe the content (to communicate about what is this project about, what technical language is required), the physical set-ups (to talk about how we will work together to do this, what resources and materials is required), and the relational arrangements (to discuss who is working with whom, what grouping arrangements, who is leading). Alena, the teachers, and students at the school developed a 'shared' language that was relevant and appropriate to their particular classroom contexts and to the particular curriculum they were working with. Different conceptualisations, and ways of thinking and using language, enable and constrain different ways of teaching and learning, and are encountered as particular *cultural-discursive* arrangements.

In this realm, it is the role of the middle leader to not only understand the kinds of language and discourses needed for themselves, but find ways to bring others into the semantic space towards collective meaning making and comprehensivity.

Opening up physical spaces

In the *physical space-time* of meetings, workshops, seminars, interclass visits, or professional conversations or lessons in classrooms, we may observe (empirically) different *activities* taking place. Different physical set-ups, resources, and materials will be required on different days in different professional learning episodes with different purposes or agendas. Each differently influencing the ways of *doing* an activity. Middle leaders may for example arrange how the teachers, students, and the resources and materials – as entities which co-inhabit the space of the classroom – will work together at the time.

For example, at Bushland Primary School Alena was conscious of the ways that different physical set-ups, activities, or materials enable and constrain different ways of doing things. Even the ways desks, people, and resources were arranged or distributed made the different activities and relationships between the teachers and between her and colleagues possible. These particular aspects of the physical space-time are encountered as *material-economic* arrangements.

In this realm, to open up and bring others into the physical space-time, the role of the middle leader is to understand and be overtly conscious of how different configurations of people, activities, and materials in the space influences what happens at the time.

Opening up social spaces

In the *social space* of leading professional learning, teachers and middle leaders generally experience different ways of relating to one another (like expert-novice, peers or colleagues, mentor-mentee, facilitator-learner). These ways of relating reflect and affect different kinds of relationships that influence personal agency, power, and solidarity among those present.

For example, at Bushland Primary School, Alena organised teachers to work together in a range of different ways including as the whole school group or in small groups, in teaching teams or in one-on-one sessions. These involved different variations of autonomous activity and collaboration that formed the sociality of the practice. Different ways of relating formed particular *social-political arrangements* that served to play part in the development of the particular roles and relationships teachers encountered at the school.

In this realm, it is the role of the middle leader to be conscious of the roles and the relationships between people. It is also necessary to consider how their practices form and inform different kinds of participation rights and how these enable and constrain different kinds of leading, teaching, and learning roles and relationships between the people (teachers and middle leaders) involved.

The practice architectures that support and challenge middle leading

Middle leading is a social practice; thus, requires a social theory of practice to understand it then develop it further. In a broad sense, practising practices like middle leading, requires a theory (a notion, idea, or conceptualisation) that illuminates and brings meaning and coherence to:

- the sociality of practices;
- what practices are comprised of;
- the conditions that enable and constrain the conduct of practices as it happens in particular sites;
- the shaping dimensions of practices;
- the relationship(s) between practices; and
- the alignments, synergies, tensions, and contestation between practices.

Specifically, for framing and conceptualising middle leading, it is necessary to understand:

- what middle leading practices are comprised of;
- the historical, experiential, political, and local conditions that enable and constrain the conduct of middle leading *as it happens* in particular sites;
- the shaping dimensions or practice architectures of middle leading;
- the relationship(s) between middle leading practices and other practices like student learning needs, teaching and pedagogies, the kind of professional learning already present, the leading practices of others and the broader research, political and curriculum agendas influencing the work in schools; and
- the alignments, synergies, tensions, and contestation between specific site-based practices related to student learning, teaching, professional learning and development, leading, evaluating, and researching.

As introduced previously, a useful theoretical tool for understanding the work of middle leaders is 'the theory of practice architectures' (Kemmis et al., 2014) and 'the theory of ecologies of practices' (Kemmis et al., 2012). The latter explains the existence and development of, and the dynamic interdependency between, education practices. It is a way of thinking about practices that considers how they relate to one another, like the ways that teaching practices are intimately connected to students' learning practices in classrooms or the ways that leading practices are tightly related to professional learning practices in a school. Together, the theory of practice architectures and ecologies of practices offer theoretical tools to show how middle leading practices are fundamentally *site-based*, interdependent with, and interconnected to other education practices, and importantly need to be understood, developed, and practised in integrated and related ways in school sites.

Why theory to understand practice?

Briefly, theories provide a systematic and logical way of understanding and representing the conditions and circumstances in which the social, physical, and political world exists. In educational work, understanding the practices, behaviours, dispositions, conditions, and/or situations of the people involved is necessary for framing, conceptualising, and reframing (and transforming) what happens in places where education practices happen. We stress that any theory of practice must be a theory of social life, since practices are constituted in and for the social world. Therefore, any practice theory must also liberate the entangled dimensions of the social world to offer ways to reasonably understand the multidimensionality, interrelatedness, and complexity of practices. Thus, going beyond a rhetorical understanding of education practices requires a theory of practice that allows us to 'get at' the density, permeability, and nuances of practical work.

Getting to a theory of social practice

Practices are always enacted in nuanced ways. This is because practices are both situated (happen somewhere in real time) and socially constructed by human beings who come together as individuals in particular sites (like classrooms or family gatherings or football matches) and under particular circumstances (like in lessons, mealtimes, or training). In many ways, practices are organised and cohere around the everyday ordinariness (sometimes take-for-grantedness) of day-to-day life. At the same time practices are transient or fleeting in nature as they pass through or unfold (as we suggest) through particular moments of time (in a meeting or a lesson). The conduct of everyday practices, thus, can be understood in routines, predictability, and order. But be prepared for the extraordinary and unexpected at the same time (because it is always an open question about how things will actually unfold or happen in real life in real time). This means *practices are pre-figured but not pre-determined*. This duality requires a critical stance. This is true for understanding middle leading practices.

Fundamentally, middle leading is a social practice because it always involves working with other people. So, as practitioners of education practices, middle leaders – in the company of colleagues in professional learning meetings *or* in the company of students in lessons – practise practices every day as a teacher, leader, professional developer, learner, colleague (Edwards-Groves and Rönnerman, 2012). As suggested, in reality, practising practices is never neutral but always undergirded by prior experiences of all practitioners involved as well as pre-existing ideas, ideologies, traditions of the field, discipline knowledge, standards, curriculums, policy agendas, and so on. We describe this as the *pre-figurement of practices*. However, we also know that enacting practices (in the moment) is not only influenced by what pre-exists, but by what is brought into the site (like resources, ideas, policies, language) and who is present at the time (like students, other teachers, colleagues, the principal) and the relationships (in terms of the agency, solidarity, and power) between them. Each of these dimensions of practice influence or prefigure the happenings, but do not necessarily determine what actually happens at the time. This why we said that practices are always pre-figured, but not pre-determined.

This means that in actual sites, practices are always influenced by other things that are both local and external, that both enable and constrain what can possibly be done. That is to say, practices of any kind are influenced by conditions we describe as *practice architectures*. The theory of practice architectures and ecologies of practices (Kemmis et al., 2014) lead educators towards a theory of social practice that enables us to consider broader questions concerning the:

- *cultural-discursive, material-economic*, and *social-political* arrangements (or practice architectures) that shape the practices for changing educational practices in schools;
- distinctive and interrelated ways education practices in schools are intricately and ecologically connected with one another;
- nuanced ways practices are enacted, changing, and changed in schools;
- practices and the practice architectures that influence the change process 'as it is experienced by practitioners' in the school;
- ways that middle leading is a practice architecture for other practices in the school;
- sustainability of practices; and
- consequences for the lifeworlds of middle leaders, teachers, leaders, and students as they variously negotiate, take on board, or contest changes to everyday teaching and learning practices in their particular site.

The theory of practice architectures, described above, positions the focus on middle leading as orienting towards *educational praxis*. In this book, we lay this as the foundation for thinking about how middle leading works in local school development as practice that creates:

- educationally right action for the formation of individuals and the development of good communities;
- a public arena for intellectual engagement with educational topics – whatever the discipline area;
- the space for rigorous thinking, inquiry talk, deepening reasoning, critical reflection, and collective problem solving;
- spaces for coming to clarity and shared understandings among professionals in the school; and
- inclusive, scaffolded, and collaborative spaces for focused professional learning.

It is important, therefore, that the middle leader understand what this means for them as they deploy their leading in practices.

A theory-of-practice-for-action

Part of the work of the middle leader is the need to develop a strong sense of what theories and actions shape their own practices; we describe this as developing *a theory-of-practice-for-action* (Edwards-Groves and Davidson, 2017). This means from the outset it is necessary for the middle leader to identify and potentially name the concepts, schematics, principles, or beliefs that influence and shape their own educational teaching and learning practices and trace these back to some basic theoretical propositions. We see this as a necessary early step, since to support teachers' learning and change requires an overt knowledge of one's own theories of action; that is, to more explicitly understand the concepts and ideas that underpin their day-to-day teaching decisions and practices in action. So, when a person acts, does or practises something, there are presuppositions or ideas, previous knowledge and experiences, that influence their practising.

Therefore, to reframe and then transform practices requires noticing and naming the practices being practised (Edwards-Groves and Davidson, 2017). With time and experience practitioners, like middle leaders, thereby need to develop understandings about their practices in explicit ways; for us this means a meta-awareness of their theories-of-practice-in-action that both inform and shape practices in their practising. Some describe this as practical wisdom.

To change practices, we also know that practices cannot remain static, that things need to be different going forward. For the middle leader this means considering the practices as well as the practice architectures that need to also change (because practices are always influenced by practice architectures). For example, if a teachers' goal is to help students develop participation skills in class discussions, then the teacher might need to change the physical set-ups (or material-economic arrangements) in the room; for instance they might have the students seated in a circle or in small group structures rather than in a cohort facing the teacher at the front of the room. This means it is important to know that to change practices requires changing the practice architectures. Consequently, part of the process for pedagogical change requires middle leaders supporting teachers to come to know their own practices for themselves and to understand the practice architectures (conditions) that are enabling and constraining their work. This means providing ways that assist teachers:

- Identify and understand the enabling and constraining conditions that influence their teaching and their students' learning;
- Notice and see their practices for themselves;
- Relate the change agenda to their own site and circumstances;
- Change it (the sayings, doings, and relatings) for themselves; and
- Design and adjust their professional learning (or for example in CPAR) projects for themselves (Edwards-Groves and Davidson, 2017).

Each of these actions imply pedagogical praxis. For us, leading wisely forms critical pedagogical praxis (necessary for improving student learning and professional learning), it is a condition that holds the integrity of middle leading practice together. It is what we consider to be wise, ethical and prudent action, that which is right to do for those present at the time, and given the circumstances bearing down on the sayings, doings, and relatings of practice (Edwards-Groves and Grootenboer, 2015). This means that the middle leader accepts the teacher's right and responsibility to make decisions about their professional learning and practice development, never losing sight of their commission to assist teachers develop and fulfil their own theory-of-action-in-practice. For the middle leader, this means managing the delicate balance between achieving the school's policy and development agenda and working toward an individual teacher's own development plan.

Conclusion

The position on practice, practice architectures and theory of practice for action presented in this chapter shows that it is nonsensical at anything other than the most broad and general level, to talk about *best practice* as if it can be relevant to different schools, departments, groups, and contexts. In essence, this is because, as we suggest, practices are made and remade in every site every time. Understanding the dimensions of middle leading as practice, as we outlined through the lens of practice architectures and ecologies of practices, will help middle leaders become overtly conscious of what forms, informs, and transforms practices in schools. It is hoped that these theories equip you, as the middle leader, with theoretical tools to lead and facilitate practical change and development in ways that respond to the circumstances and needs of your school. We envisage that the theoretical propositions we presented will provide you with the recognition that to change practices by supporting the practice development of colleagues requires a site-based (or ontological) understanding of the work you do.

Theory-into-practice (TIPs): questions for reflection and discussion

In this chapter we have outlined a theoretical understanding of practice to underpin our understanding of middle leading. In summary, to change practices requires changing the practice architectures. This means middle leaders need to know:

i   that *practices* are made up of *sayings* (evident in one's thinking and words, in language and discourses), *doings* (evident in one's activities, use of materials and physical space in time), and *relatings* (evident in one's relationships and way of relating to others);
ii that *practice architectures* are the conditions that enable and constrain what happens in practices; and that these are influenced by cultural-discursive, material-economic, and social-political arrangements that exist in a place where educational practices happen; and
iii the ways that education practices are interrelated (like in an ecology);

iv critical pedagogical praxis is necessary FOR student learning, FOR professional learning, and FOR leading;
v that for pedagogical change, middle leaders need to support teachers to:

*develop a theory-of-practice-in-action;
*notice and name, or learn and see, it for themselves;
*relate the practice change to their site and circumstances;
*change it for themselves; and
*design their professional learning (or CPAR) projects for themselves.

vi Consider how the ideas presented about this theory can help you make sense of your educational practices? Note these.
vii If you consider educational development in your school site, what might the new (or modified) practices *sound like (sayings)? look like (doings)? feel like (relatings)?* Use this Y chart (Figure 2.5) to guide your thinking about practices?

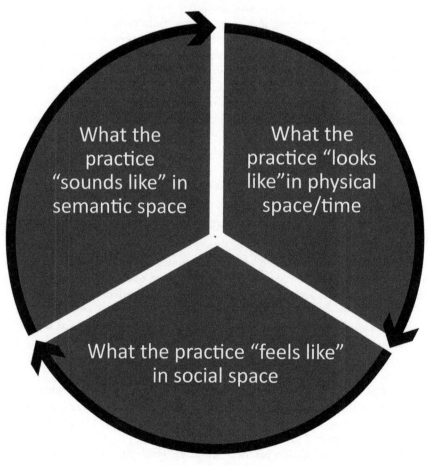

Figure 2.5 Y chart

- What are the sayings (languages and discourse) of the practice?
- What are the doings (activities and resources) of the practice?
- What are the relatings (interactions and types of relationships) of the practice?

1. Can you identify the *practice architectures* that enable and constrain your middle leading practices? How do these shape your educational practices in your school site? Can you shape them so your leading is more productive and effective?
2. As a middle leader your practices create the practice architectures for your colleagues teaching practices. How are you enabling (and constraining) effective pedagogical practices in your school site?
3. As you support teachers develop *a theory-of-practice-for-action* for focusing and directing their professional learning, consider yours by asking the question: what is your *theory-of-practice-for-action?*
4. While many systemic leaders and bureaucrats are looking to implement *best practice*, we have suggested that such a thing does not exist, because practices need to be made and remade in each unique site. We suggest a better aspiration might be *promising practices*. Discuss 'best practice' and 'promising practice' as it might be understood and used in your school site.

References

Edwards Groves, C. and Rönnerman, K. (2012). 'Generating leading practices through professional learning', *Professional Development in Education*, 39(1), 122–140.

Edwards-Groves, C. and Grootenboer, P. (2015). 'Practice and praxis in literacy education', *Australian Journal of Language and Literacy*, 38(3), 150–161.

Edwards-Groves, C. and Davidson, C. (2017). *Becoming a Meaning Maker: Talk and Interaction in the Dialogic Classroom*. Sydney, NSW: Primary English Teaching Association Australia (PETAA).

Grootenboer, P. (2018). *The practices of school middle leadership: Leading professional learning*. Singapore: Springer Education.

Kemmis, S. (2018). Life in Practices: Challenges for Education and Educational Research. In C. Edwards-Groves, P. Grootenboer and J. Wilkinson (Eds), *Education in an Era of Schooling: Critical perspectives of Educational Practice and Action Research. A Festschrift for Stephen Kemmis* (pp. 239–254). Singapore: Springer.

Kemmis, S., Edwards-Groves, C., Wilkinson, J. and Hardy, I. (2012). Ecologies of practices. In P. Hagar, A. Leeand A. Reich (Eds), *Practice, learning and change* (pp. 33–49). Dordrecht: Springer.

Kemmis, S., Wilkinson, J., Edwards-Groves, C., Hardy, I., Grootenboer, P. and Bristol, L. (2014). *Changing Practices, Changing Education*. Singapore: Springer Education.

Further reading

Ministry of Education. (2012). *Leading from the Middle: educational leadership for middle and senior leaders*. Wellington, NZ: Learning Media.

3 School-based professional learning and development

It is important to understand and grow professional learning and curriculum development at the local level – in schools and classrooms. This is not to deny that there are programmes and changes that are initiated at a national level (e.g. the Australian curriculum), state level (e.g. assessment and teacher accreditation processes), district level, or even within a system, but rather to acknowledge that all these changes, programmes, initiatives, or requirements must be *actioned* in schools and classrooms. While a politician or a bureaucrat may initiate something (e.g. a new curriculum), and district, university, or school leaders may then carry it forward, it is actually teachers who will ultimately have to enact it with students in classrooms.

This is a profound point because it means that whatever happens above, before, and beyond the classroom – where students and teachers meet around a curriculum, is always mediated through the local pedagogical practices of the classroom teacher. Of course, there are a range of factors that impact on students' capacity to learn and engage with the curriculum in the classroom (e.g. family life), but all the goals and purposes of the *education system* are channelled through the classroom teacher. To this end, Grootenboer (2018) commented:

> While acknowledging that learning occurs everywhere and through many modes, in schools the key site is the classroom. The classroom is where all the intentions and requirements of the curriculum meet learners, and it is where the impact of decisions made at all the levels of leadership from the local school to the federal government have to be interpreted and enacted for the formation of individuals and communities. With this in mind, it is not surprising that a range of studies have found that the most significant factor in the effectiveness of education is the teacher. Generally, and primarily, it is the teacher that has to mediate, interpret, and enact educational policies, programmes, and procedures in the classroom to provide learning opportunities for students. The teacher is the interface between the curriculum and learners, and so whatever is discussed and decided *prior* to the classroom site, it is always mediated through the teacher.
>
> (italics in original, p. 4)

To this end, considering the site of the teacher practising in classrooms is of critical importance. This means that if we want to provide the best education for students, then the key factor is the teacher and what happens in classrooms. With this in mind, we believe that the main focus of educational development needs to be practices of the classroom, and that professional learning and curriculum development are crucial *at the local level*. Furthermore, this is important then because such development can be responsive to unique and particular educational needs and requirements of the students and the community. It is obvious then, that middle leaders, who practise their leading in and around classrooms, are best placed to lead this educational development, because they have an intimate understanding and close proximity to the *hot site of education* – the classroom.

This idea has some significant implications for schools and how education is developed at all levels. First, it would seem important that when national, state, or system reforms are initiated, that more emphasis and support is afforded to those leading and enacting the reforms in schools and classrooms – i.e. middle leaders and teachers. Second, in schools, middle leaders need to be supported and equipped to lead educational development, and their roles need to be primarily defined to this end, so they can lead professional learning and curriculum development, not just help manage the administrative load of the school. Third, if education is to be developed, then teachers need time, space, and resources to focus on teaching and learning – currently they seem to be required to spend much of their time on administrative and compliance tasks rather than centring on their *core business* of teaching in the classroom.

We make a strong case for school-based professional learning and curriculum development, and now we turn to how a middle leader can lead and facilitate such development. Of course, having made the case that educational development needs to site-based and responsive to local needs and conditions, we cannot now provide a universal set of procedures or a 'how-to-do-it recipe'. We do, however, provide some practical ideas and practices that can be reformed in different settings, and a few short *stories from practice* to show how others have undertaken this leading. Primarily we see action research as a way to organise and structure this development.

Leading educational development through action research

Action research has many forms and guises, and it has been used in sectors such as education and health to promote change through collaborative knowledge building. In short, here we see it as an on-going and sustainable way to develop educational practice collaboratively in response to local needs and conditions based on evidence. It is a way of developing pedagogy and curriculum *from the classroom out*, as opposed to the normal processes of imposing change from outside and above (or at least to develop classroom-based responses to externally required change). Action research is a way to understand your practices, and the conditions and arrangements that enable and constrain those practices, and importantly, to change and develop those practices and the allied practice conditions (Carr and Kemmis, 1986).

Action research has historically been conceptualised as a series of on-going cycles, with each cycle involving planning, acting, collecting evidence, and reflecting on the evidence, before then moving onto the next cycle with replanning, etc. (see Figure 3.1 below).

While this structure is useful, it is not the process of going through the cycles *per se* that is action research, but rather, the format, which can be modified to suit local needs and conditions, that facilitates evidence-based change (Kemmis, McTaggart and Nixon, 2014). Also, in this figure it looks as if each aspect is distinct, but in practice this is not usually this clear cut, as, for example, observation or evidence gathering often occurs at the same time as the action. That is, in practice, inquiry through action research is recursive. However, what is clear is that:

- planning for the subsequent cycle does not emerge until after reflecting on the evidence from the current cycle (i.e. several cycles of action research are not established in advance);
- that each cycle involves making small changes and collecting simple evidence about what happens;
- reflection is based on simple evidence that is gathered in the site; and
- the process needs to be collegial.

To illustrate an example from physical education is briefly outlined below.

Stories from practice: *how much 'P' is in PE?*

At Thomas Park College, the physical education (PE) staff had a fairly traditional sports-based programme for their Year 8 classes. Each class had two one-hour classes per week, and during this time the students had to get to the PE

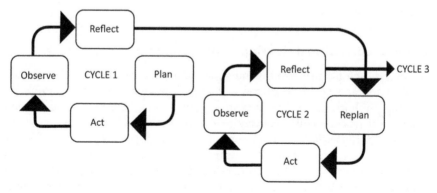

Figure 3.1 Basic action research cycles

area, change into their PE uniform, participate in the class, and then change back into their regular school clothes ready for their next class. Through dialogue at a department meeting at the start of the year, the teachers had a shared concerned about how much time the students were actually engaged in 'physical activity-based learning'. Specifically, they thought that they lost a lot of time in the 'administrative parts of the lesson' (e.g. getting changed, moving to the teaching space, marking the roll), and 'just playing games with many not participating', and so they embarked on a year-long action research project to investigate these issues and develop their teaching practices and the curriculum.

First, they just wanted to understand how they actually spent their time in their lessons, so they organised for each teacher to observe another teacher's lesson, and keep a simple time record of what actually happened. At the end of each lesson, the observer gave the record to the teacher concerned, and the teacher reflected on the evidence in a brief dialogue with the observer. At this time the observer did not *evaluate* the lesson – they simply reported and clarified what they saw vis-à-vis what actually happened in the lesson. Then, after three weeks when all teachers had been observed and had been an observer, they met in their usual department meeting time to collegially reflect on the evidence and the experience, and to plan the next cycle.

Overall, they were somewhat surprised and disappointed to see that the students spent very little time actually being active – in general about 25 per cent of the time was used for administration and management, 40 per cent for teacher talk and instruction, 15 per cent where most students were active, and 20 per cent where a few students were active (e.g. many were lined up waiting for their turn). While there were a number of things they could have focused on in their next cycle, they decided to start on the 40 per cent teacher talk and instruction, as they thought that this was within their immediate capacity to change. Specifically, they decided to be 'tighter and more focused in their instruction' for the skills for the next unit on soccer, and to this end, they prepared two to four key points for each instructional episode. This cycle, due to timetabling constraints, they 'put the stopwatch' on their own instruction and noted the times over the unit.

As they continued through the year the PE department went through eight 'cycles' of action research, with an extended department retreat (half day) in the middle of the year and at the end of the year, to reflect on how far they had come and to consider what they might focus on in the next year. In brief, over the year they developed their pedagogy, so they spent 'less time talking', and they also developed their curriculum so they had clearer details about the key instructional points. The middle leader was also able to convince the school senior leaders to allow students to wear their PE uniform in classes immediately before and/or after their PE lesson, so they did not lose as much learning time from their lessons. Their case to the senior leaders was based on the evidence they collected.

In the change endeavour like the one presented in this *story from practice*, teachers and middle leaders need each other to advance their learning and development. The challenge for the middle leader is thus twofold: teachers must see themselves as action researchers with a stake in the initiative, and the middle leader must accept that teachers have to address and respond to real issues in real classrooms in real time. For change to occur, both must accept that only by challenging one's own practices. As we move on in this chapter, we will draw more on this illustrative example as we outline how middle leaders can lead curriculum development and professional learning in their own schools.

Initiating action research

In the *story from practice* above, the action research was initiated by a broad shared concern about the amount of time students were 'physical' in physical education lessons, and from this they could then start to investigate their relevant educational practices. However, the identification and shared appreciation of this first issue or concern can take time and requires collegiality. Building professional collaboration and trust are discussed in more depth in Chapter 4.

One way to prompt reflection about current practices is to take time to stop and consider what is happening, and this needs to occur outside the usual pressures of teaching in day-to-day school life. Specifically, it can be easy to get caught up with maintaining the practices that have come to characterise normal teaching and learning, but here we need to step outside the routine and consider how these sedimented ways of doing things are working. For example, a school may be teaching Roman numerals to their Year 6 students because they had traditionally always done so, and it was not until they stepped outside the usual teaching programme that they could consider whether it was still relevant or necessary.

Once a conducive time and space is found, those involved need to be able to discuss issues and ideas in a collegially respectful and open dialogue. There are many ways a leader can organise and facilitate this sort of discussion, but below we outline some steps that we have seen work in a range of context – of course these can be modified to suit your situation:

1 Through an open discussion, develop a group mind-map in response to a question like: 'What are we doing here?'; or, 'What are we concerned about?'. From this, try and identify the one concern that is shared by all. In the example above, there could have been a range of issues (e.g. students' general fitness), but they decided that their main concern was about physical education lessons not being 'physical enough'.
2 Now develop another mind-map that focuses on the identified shared concern, and again consider questions like: 'What is happening here?'; and 'What do we want to change or develop?'. From this come to a consensus about what one aspect you will develop first. Again, referencing the PE case, this would be to have students being more physically active in their learning in their physical education lessons

3   Once the single initial focus is nominated, turn this into a question that centres on action. For example, 'How can we get students more actively engaged in physical education lessons?'.
4   And then a small, manageable aspect is selected for the first cycle – this will not fully address, answer, or 'rectify' the question or concern, but it will be the start of an on-going learning and development process. Above, the first step was to collect data about how they actually spent their time in their PE lessons.

So, to lead curriculum and professional development in your school site, it is important to collegially find a shared issue or area of concern, and then collaboratively narrow that down so you can actually start with something small and doable.

Sustaining action research

The role of the middle leader is crucial in establishing an action research project, but it requires a different form of leading practice to sustain it. As we have seen across many educational sites, there can be initial enthusiasm and commitment to investigating pedagogical practices, but after time the activities and pressures of regular school life can see the initial impetus dissipate – maintaining and continuing the normal routines and practices of school life result in the change and development initiatives being squeezed out. So, not surprisingly, the main reason touted is a lack of time! This requires the middle leader to manage and facilitate conditions so time is available.

Of course, the way that educational development can be sustained through action research will depend on a range of factors and conditions, but the main task of the middle leader will be to plan for focused professional learning time. This is important so teachers and middle leaders can move beyond just repeating the same practices and routines that they have already been doing, and instead, develop their practices. In the *story from practice* below, Monique outlines how she made space and time for their action research as part of her primary school syndicate routine.

Stories from practice: *doing meetings differently*

Monique was the leader of the Year 2 and 3 syndicate in a medium-sized primary school, and she, with her four teaching colleagues, had initiated an action research approach to investigate and develop their teaching and learning of spelling. After some enthusiasm and a flurry of activity at the start that saw them quickly move through the first cycle, Monique noted that 'things were starting to slip as people became busy' and other more 'routine' things were prioritised. She acknowledged that school life was very busy, and Monique was also concerned that she did not want to add to the teachers' stress levels, or demand more of their time. However, she was also committed to the on-going professional learning of her teaching staff, and responsive curriculum development.

As the middle leader, Monique decided to change the structure and focus of their fortnightly syndicate meetings in order to facilitate the action research. Previously, these 75-minute meetings had been held in her classroom preparation area, and the agenda had largely been concerned with disseminating information on managerial and administrative matters. Monique decided to use electronic means to share most of the administrative information, and to deal with other relevant matters with the appropriate teachers outside the meeting, so the meeting time could be devoted to the action research. She commented:

> I wanted our own learning as teachers to be central – as educators it is important that we are also learners! So by starting with the professional development stuff we were showing that it was important. ... Actually, it became easy to manage the 'administrivia' as well this way, so that was a bonus!

Also, to develop a more dialogic and collegial culture in the meetings, Monique had it move around each of the teachers' classrooms, and she ensured that some simple refreshments were provided.

Developing pedagogy, curriculum, and the conditions for change

In the brief example above, the teachers wanted to develop their pedagogy and the curriculum, but as the middle leader Monique needed to change the conditions of their work so this could happen. Similarly, in the first *story from practice* the middle leader organised a change in the arrangements of their work (i.e. timetabling) which facilitated a continuation of their educational development in the PE department. The point here is that it is not enough to just look to change practices – there needs to be concurrent attention to changing the conditions and arrangements (practice architectures) that enable and constrain the practices, as this is a crucial leading role for middle leaders.

While this may seem like common sense, it is a particularly important point when engaging in site-based education development. Put simply, this means asking key questions when starting or revising action research-based curriculum development and professional learning:

1 What practices do we want to develop? And why?
2 What conditions and arrangements enable and constrain these practices?

It is difficult to revise and grow pedagogy and curriculum if the educational conditions and arrangements remain the same, so these things can, and need to be, developed concurrently. For example, if there was an aim to develop the curriculum and pedagogy to include more digital tools, then there would also be a need for appropriate hardware and software, and also the necessary technical support, but also teacher training and development that not only focused on the required knowledge, but also aspects like the teacher's confidence. Without allied attention to the practices AND the enabling and constraining conditions, the educational development is likely to be compromised and to struggle.

Action research – from a project to practices

Throughout this chapter, as we have discussed action research it has probably sounded like contained and discrete projects – you have an issue or concern, you proceed through a series of 'action research cycles' over a set period of time (e.g. one year), and then it is wrapped-up and everyone moves on. Indeed, this is often how departments, schools, syndicates, and groups of teachers start school-based educational development, but we think it has far greater educational potential when middle leaders see action research as the way of operating and collaborating together.

It seems that teachers and schools are being inundated by a continuous stream of new innovations and programmes to address a raft of concerns, and often in response to the latest political issue or educational fad. This can result in an inconsistent and incoherent sequence of professional development events that leads to little educational change, but often creates 'innovation fatigue'. The disappointing thing about this is that the very ones who are the promoters and 'providers' of education – teachers and schools, end up with impoverished and ineffective learning themselves. For this reason, in this chapter and throughout this book, we have promoted middle leaders as the ones who lead the curriculum development and professional learning of their teaching peers, and the best way to do this is through ongoing collaborative action research, in response to the needs of their school site (rather than the latest fad or initiative that may come from outside the school).

To this end, we make the following simple practical points:

- The team of teachers needs to devote most of its administrative time (e.g. department meetings) to focus on their learning (i.e. professional and curriculum development). These ideas have been picked up recently in the concept of *Professional Learning Communities* (PLCs).
- Having an action research 'project' to initiate this way of working together is a good way for a middle leader to initiate school-based educational development. While the initial attention of those involved will be on the focus topic or issue, the middle leader can simultaneously use it to build a new way of working together based on ongoing collaborative action research.
- Although the cycles of action research are ongoing, it is important to stop for a good period of time (half to a full day) every half-year to reflect on your learning and change, and to reset your sails for the next six months.

An ongoing culture built around continuous development through action research creates a good way to integrate and support new team members into the department or group. Finally, we need to add a final, but important consideration about maintaining a critical perspective. To illustrate this point, a *story from practice* is provided below.

Keeping a critical perspective

In Australia the mathematical outcomes for Indigenous[1] learners are significantly lower than for the non-Indigenous population, and this is, to a degree, because the mathematics education they have experienced has not connected to their identities, histories, or ways of learning. The story reported here comes from one secondary school which was involved in a large national project to improve mathematical pedagogy in order to realise better learning outcomes for these Indigenous students who had not previously been served well by the mainstream teaching practices. Specifically, this *story from practice* focuses on a middle leader – Simon, the Head of Mathematics, as he sought to work with his teaching staff to promote more open-ended investigative teaching practices that related to the students' lives and interests. Simon and his teachers used action research to try these new approaches and to see how they went.

The teachers in this mathematics department were generally keen and enthusiastic about developing more engaging strategies into their mathematics teaching, and they had decided together to start their action research by each implement a common task into their lessons with the Year 9 (aged 14–15 years) classes. Teachers then collected some evidence related to the task including student work samples and personal reflections. This then became the evidence that was brought forward to the next action research meeting where they collectively reflected on the tasks, the engagement of their Indigenous students, and the teaching approach in order to plan the next cycle.

However, while there was general enthusiasm and interest, one of the teachers (Donna) was less positive and confident about the approach. Because the teaching group had decided to take this plan, she agreed to try, but she was not convinced that it would work – particularly with the Indigenous students. After implementing the activity in her class, Donna commented:

> I tried the activity as we all agreed, but I knew that it wouldn't work because these students [in a lower ability class] can't cope without the structure of a formal lesson ... When I think about this lesson it would never work because they need it to be more controlled.

What was interesting was that while the activity was productive and seemed to move the general mathematics teaching approach of the department towards something that was more engaging for the Indigenous (and other learners), this was not the case for Donna.

This created an awkward situation for Simon as the middle leader, and he was concerned about how he could maintain the momentum of the action research project in a participatory, but also critical manner. He said:

> I appreciate that Donna wants to be a team player and be involved, but she doesn't really try and change or give it a chance. Her ideas seem very fixed and so I don't think she will ever change. So as the HoD [middle leader] should I force her to try these changes, or am I just 'banging my head on a brick wall'? Is it possible to have everyone participating in these action research projects if they don't really want to try, reflect, and change?

Simon has posed some interesting questions that underpin one of the dilemmas for middle leaders. Donna's case shows how an uncritical perspective can result in simplifying the agenda by just confirming already pre-existing ideas and practices, and the re-enforcement of what was already being thought and done. This raises questions about whether Donna was 'participating' in the action research processes if she was unwilling to actually critically reflect on her teaching practice, and legitimately or genuinely seeking to change.

The purpose of this *story from practice* is to show that, despite most the accounts that are presented in books and seminars, leading development in a school is never easy or straight-forward, and if it is undertaken in an unreflective and uncritical way, then it can lead to the ill-informed reinforcement of already held views and practices. Thus, for middle leaders, being 'critical' is not something abstract nor about criticising per se, but rather it is about using evidence to really look at what goes on in our actual classrooms and schools, and in the light of that evidence, developing more effective and inclusive practices.

Conclusion

The foundational focus of this book is about middle leadership and leading curriculum development and professional learning. In this chapter we have focused specifically on how this can be undertaken in school sites. Indeed, we have strongly contended that to be effective educational development needs to be school-based, and driven by middle leaders in response to local needs and conditions – 'classroom-out' reform rather than top-down imposed change. This is because education – learning and teaching, actually happens in classrooms where teachers and students engage in the curriculum together. But this requires middle leaders to move beyond just managing and organising the educational practices that already exist and prevail. It demands middle leaders who can facilitate evidence-based, site-responsive educational development, and we have suggested that this can be organised and facilitated through action research.

Theory-into-practice (TIPs): questions for reflection and discussion

1. In your role do you see yourself more as a manager/administrator or a professional leader?

    a How much of your time as a middle leader is spent in administration and management?

    b How much time and energy is spent leading professional learning and curriculum development?

2. What might be some of the compelling issues or concerns for your department, faculty, syndicate or school?

    a Would these issues or concerns be shared by your teaching colleagues?

    b What might be the *shared* issues or concerns?

    c What would be the associated conditions and arrangements that enable and constrain that you will need to simultaneously consider?

3. How could you facilitate action research in your teacher team?

    a How can you get your colleagues on board?

Note

1 We acknowledge that the term 'Indigenous' is a homogenising term for a range of different Aboriginal and Torres Strait Island peoples, but it used here for ease of understanding for an international audience.

References

Carr, W. and Kemmis, S. (1986). *Becoming Critical: Education, Knowledge and Action Research*. London: Falmer Press.

Grootenboer, P. (2018). *The practices of school middle leadership: Leading professional learning*. Singapore: Springer.

Kemmis, S., McTaggart, R. and Nixon, R. (2014). *The action research planner. Doing critical participatory action research*. Singapore: Springer.

Wooden, J. (1997). *A Lifetime of Observations and Reflections On and Off the Court*. New York: McGraw-Hill Professional. www.movemequotes.com/top-15-john-wooden-quotes/.

4 Relating, trust, and dialogic practice in middle leading

In this chapter we provide a robust and deep discussion of two related key issues in middle leading – relational trust and professional dialogues. First, we focus on trust. For us it is the 'glue' that holds a department or team together. Second, we show how trust can be nourished through dialogic practices which, for us, form conditions for communities of learning and professional practice to be enabled. As teachers engage in professional development, they are particularly vulnerable, and so need trust to function in open and generative ways; it needs to be present and ultimately to fulfil the promise of professional development as a mechanism to progress education. Developing professionally means considering the conditions that generate and foster teacher commitment, communication, community, collaboration, care, and consistency. Our research has shown that when teachers talk with one another about their practices, they are creating a dialogic space that not only sets up conditions for deepening their understandings but, at the same time, these conditions create a relational space that make trust possible. The reciprocity between relational trust and dialogic approaches to professional learning are explored in detail in this chapter.

Relational trust

High leverage leading requires relational trust. Relational trust is a concept often described in the literature as a necessary condition for schools; particularly in establishing and sustaining communities of practices and for accomplishing professional development. In this chapter, we propose that the repertoire of dialogic practices, described in the subsequent section, create the kind of communicative space that engenders relationships where trust builds. But, as we have found (Edwards-Groves, Grootenboer and Rönnerman, 2016), relational trust, at its core, is multidimensional and multilayered. Successful middle leaders foster relational trust on five fronts: interpersonal trust, interactional trust, intersubjective trust, intellectual trust, and pragmatic trust. An overview of these five dimensions is presented in the extensive Tables 4.1–4.5 below (adapted from Edwards-Groves, Grootenboer and Rönnerman, 2016).

Table 4.1 Interpersonal trust

Trust dimension	Middle leading practices	Testimonials
in and for an open, democratic, communicative space	**what we say, do and how we relate to others**	**what teachers and principals say about middle leaders**
Interpersonal trust *in and for social space* What conditions do I create that promotes inclusivity? Fosters a shared responsibility to the professional learning community? Facilitates teacher capacity?	**As a middle leader do I...?** act as a leader; demonstrate ways of relating that are open, inclusive, and respectful of all teacher learning needs and styles; get to really know my teachers; connect with others at a personal level; instil confidence and motivation in others; demonstrate mutual respect, care, and empathetic understanding; instil a sense of belonging; display a mutual recognition that we are all learners together; and *am I* recognised as trustworthy, and is trusting and entrusted (by the principal, the teachers, and others, with whom they work) with the responsibility to lead teacher professional learning.	We trust her; she gets our issues; she is genuinely interested in us; we respect her and she respects us; she takes us from where we are; she is not judgemental; I feel a part of the whole thing; she is open; she encourages us; connects with us at a personal level; reliable; helps to keep us focused and motivated; she is so generous with her time and with her knowledge; she cares, and you can tell; her natural enthusiasm is attractive for helping us build and grow together; she is so approachable.

commitment–communication–community–collegiality–collaboration–care–consistency

Interpersonal trust concerns the way middle leaders demonstrate empathy, relate to, respect and engender confidence in their teaching peers through their close interpersonal interactions.

Interactional trust relates to the way middle leaders operate from a listening stance, and so open up and sustain safe spaces for communication, collaboration and democratic dialogues. Through these interactions middle leaders, in the company of peers, collectively engage in activities that promote encouragement, clarification, advice giving and problem-solving.

Intersubjective trust is demonstrated in the way middle leaders display genuine 'withness' and collegiality through joining others to establish shared meanings by participating in shared language, activities and community. Intersubjective spaces are those dimensions of social practices created by people as they come together as interlocutors in actions and interactions. Through these actions and interactions, people create *semantic* spaces, *physical* spaces and *social* spaces to understand and grow one another – that is, create communicative spaces for intersubjective meaning making.

Table 4.2 Interactional trust

Trust dimension	Middle leading practices	Testimonials
in and for an open, democratic, communicative space	*what we say, do and how we relate to others*	*what teachers and principals say about middle leaders*
Interactional trust *in and for social space* In what ways do I create conditions for open communication and interaction? Promotes teacher agency? Fosters share responsibility for substantive dialogue?	**Am I the middle leader who opens a communicative space that:** is safe and dialogic; provides opportunities to express ideas freely in a climate of trust and shared participation; enables collaboration, cooperation and professional partnerships; is a collective endeavour; provides opportunities for participants to listen to one another and consider alternative points of view, approaches and solutions; enables participants to develop their own and each other's ideas in meaningful professional conversations and thought.	We all get to have our say; we have time to think and to talk; it's a shared thing; open conversations; our professional learning conversations are kept focused, strategic, and intentional; collaborative; she listens to us even if we don't always understand or agree; the dialogue is reflective and reflexive.

commitment-communication-community-collegiality-collaboration-care-consistency

Intellectual trust involves the way middle leaders convey self-confidence, high levels of expertise and professional knowledge and practical wisdom regarding the developmental work.

Pragmatic trust refers to the way middle leaders lead change that is practical, relevant, realistic and achievable by those present. The programme agenda and timelines for example, are reasonable in light of the in situ demands that influence the complex lives of teachers and students in their day-to-day work. Because of their positioning *in the middle*, middle leaders are critical agents for facilitating and nourishing a culture of relational trust in enabling and sustainable ways.

In practice as it happens in sites, these five dimensions of relational trust are entangled with one another to create particular conditions required for creating communities of mutual support – for transformation. These conditions both form and informed by *commitment-communication-community-collegiality-collaboration-care-consistency*.

Relational trust, characterised in the five dimensions, represents the dimensionality of the security and confidence that teachers feel as they engage in professional learning. Knowing this not only allows middle leaders to consciously protect, preserve, and propagate communicative spaces for developing trust; but that trust, in turn, nourishes the conditions required for sustainable professional learning change. When one dimension is not present or is weak, then the other

52 *Relating, trust, and dialogic practice*

Table 4.3 Intersubjective trust

Trust dimension **in and for an open, democratic, communicative space**	Middle leading practices **what we say, do and how we relate to others**	Testimonials **what teachers and principals say about middle leaders**
Intersubjective trust *in and for semantic and social space* *What is my part in the PL? What am I doing myself? How do I create a physical and relational space conducive to supporting others to work together to solve professional problems? Fosters a shared responsibility to substantive reasoning about the topic or content, and fosters a shared responsibility for developing, displaying, and securing knowledge?*	**Am I the middle leader who…?** is part of the learning agenda as equally as I am part of the leading agenda; establishes shared responsibility for making meaning, coming to consensus, and decision making; takes time to listen to and learn from others so we can move forward together; creates enabling *practice architectures* (or conditions) in the range of opportunities for people to come together in professional learning activities (in physical space-time) where the conditions are democratic (in social space) and a shared language is developed (in semantic space); demonstrates *withness*, togetherness, collegiality, and cooperation; works towards solidarity and teacher agency.	She is journeying with us; learning alongside us; she makes it so we understand each other; she treats us as professional equals; walking with you every step of the way; stays the distance with us; trialling the changes with us; she always makes time for us; classroom walk-throughs helps us see the changes in real teaching; coaching conversations help me keep focused on my development; she doesn't just tell us what to do, but tries to show us ways forward that she has trialled; we are all in this together; a shared goal; she helps us develop a shared language.

commitment–communication–community–collegiality–collaboration–care–consistency

dimensions become strained, and the relationship compromised. As a middle leader, Culhanie suggests (in the following *story from practice*), recognising, understanding and developing the dimensionality of trust *is a hill worth climbing*. For her, *it is worthwhile investment, because teachers are worth investing in*. In this way, as she explains, the multiple dimensions of relational trust are mutually formational and transformational goals of teacher professional learning. As the example will show, the five dimensions of trust form interrelated social resources necessary for nurturing and securing sustainable practice development in schools.

Stories from practice: leading with sensitivity, empathy, and wisdom

Culhanie is a teaching assistant principal in a small rural school, but she describes her role as a middle leader since the main part of her role is teaching her composite Year 3/4 primary class. Culhanie worked hard to keep herself current with contemporary pedagogies through professional reading and further

Table 4.4 Intellectual trust

Trust dimension	Middle leading practices	Testimonials
in and for an open, democratic, communicative space	*what we say, do and how we relate to others*	*what teachers and principals say about middle leaders*
Intellectual trust *in and for semantic space* How well do I know the topic, material? How do I create a semantic space that develops and challenges thinking and language, and creates conditions for developing knowledge and understandings through reasoning and evidence-informed talk?	**Do others have confidence in me? Am I recognised as…?** professional; knowledgeable about the content and the material; having capacity for providing intellectual challenge and scope for extending the thinking of others; seeking betterment for myself (learner); demonstrating wisdom; one who plans for transformational work that is targeted and purposeful, having specific goals in mind related to improving student learning.	She is professional; she knows what she is talking about; she challenges us – our thinking and our practice; she reads a lot; they know what they are doing and why; pushes us to go further; she helps us develop our own personal professional theories of action; wise; the work they do shows three levels of commitment and accountability – to self-learning, to student learning and to teacher learning.

commitment-communication-community-collegiality-collaboration-care-consistency

Table 4.5 Pragmatic trust

Trust dimension	Middle leading practices	Testimonials
in and for an open, democratic, communicative space	*what you say, do and how you relate to others*	*what teachers and principals say about middle leaders*
Pragmatic trust *in and for physical space time* Is the PL relevant? Doable? Realistic? How do I create a physical space and time for professional learning?	**Do I negotiate professional learning whereby…?** the learning agenda, activities and expectations are sensible, practical and realistic; the change focus is timely and relates to the needs and circumstances of the particular context (teacher needs, school community circumstances, student learning needs, the school's professional learning plan/agenda); there is strategic intent in the change agenda that is highly relevant to the teacher participants; the timetable for change is reasonable, and enables cycles of action and change over time.	What is expected is doable, sensible, practical and realistic; she knows us and our students; she knows our issues in this community; she is flexible; the programme addresses big ticket items highly relevant for student learning; I trust her with driving the school change; she makes the learning interesting but achievable for the teachers in the school; it has to be sustainable, so no longer coming in for a one-off day.

commitment-communication-community-collegiality-collaboration-care-consistency study. She also prided herself on her capacity for sharing her learning in formal and informal ways with the other teachers on the staff (including John, the teaching principal). Culhanie's effort to develop and maintain trusting relationships with her peers is captured in her comment, 'it is a hill worth climbing because without establishing relational trust there is no cut-through, no commitment, and no effort by the teachers to develop'. She goes on to suggest, 'they have to see your investment too, that's always where I start, I try it out first, so I have something real to talk about'. As she said:

> you have to have people with you on all fronts otherwise the exercise is futile and teachers will return to the default so to say, without ever moving forward with their thinking or their development. Who is it that said 'if you do what you have always done, you'll get what you have always got'? I hold these words dear, knowing that I, too, have to change what I am doing to have teachers see that it can make a difference to the students, and to their learning too. I think this is part of the trust building. So, I see that a main part of my job is building the three Rs – relationships, relationships, relationships; being sensitive to their learning needs, even being compassionate, if that is not too strong a word. Trust in these relationships takes time, but it is worthwhile investment, because to me teachers are worth investing in. If they trust you then change will happen.

In her quite poetic words, she concludes, *trust is a seed to a* 'flourishing and strong learning culture, it feeds professional growth, but at the same time necessary for it to "spring to life"'.

In her school, Culhanie's commitment to building conditions for effective and successful professional growth does not go unnoticed by John and the other teachers in her school, Joy and Anette. In fact, to them, it is her ability to capitalise on her capacity to build strong relationships from a platform of sensitivity, empathy, expertise and practical wisdom that are central to building an ethos of professional learning among them. In a conversation, they said:

ANETTE: The way she shares I think is the way that you get change. She is doing what she expects us to do. I get the impression that she's trying to make what she's doing better as well. Probably then, someone might share back and then you can build and grow together; that's what she does help us build and grow together.
JOY: Well she's very educated too. She reads a lot.
JOHN: You need knowledge to build knowledge in others, but she is wise in a practical way too making it real for the teachers. You know connecting her learning to the kids learning.
JOY: Yeah, that's exactly right. She's that but she's also enthusiastic, she's keen, she's all for it. So, if someone's keen and enthusiastic, well you're going to try and get a bit off her.... she's reliable. So, you can go to her for advice or – and she can take it to John and can come back to you; and I trust her with that.

ANETTE: Yeah, I think that just having somebody that's dealing with the everyday issues in the classroom. They know how to make it not too unrealistic, it's gotta be reasonable in relation to time frames and so on. Because when you're not in the classroom you forget what it's like. I think it works because she is doing it too; she gets our issues because it is also relevant for her as a teacher.

JOHN: Culhanie is bringing in her own experiences of what teachers have to deal with every day; different things happening at home, at work. That's just leadership with the caring side of it, and Culhanie has that understanding. She brings that to her role in mentoring us through the PD.

For John, Joy and Anette, togetherness, care, reliability, and practical understanding coupled with deep knowledge, expertise, and wisdom characterised Culhanie's leading. For them, these features engendered leading with care (as John points out); this is the kind of empathetic leadership characterised by strong trusting interpersonal relationships that are critical for building knowledge and shifting practice. If any one of these dimensions is not recognised and nourished, then professional learning at its core may be compromised.

Educational transformation from an ethos of relational trust

Culhlanie's story illustrates that it is trust, made present and real in these five dimensions, that form the interrelated social resources necessary for nurturing and securing sustainable practice development in schools. On this standpoint, relational trust as is it experienced in these five dimensions addresses the vulnerability of professional learning; and importantly taking these dimensions together, relational trust is congenial to the sensitivities of change through creating safe trusting conditions for free, open, and self-critical discussions about practices (Kemmis, McTaggart and& Nixon, 2014). Educational transformation, therefore, is made possible since,

> professional learning and teacher development is compromised wherever the relational dimension in educational practice is not properly attended; that indeed, failure to attend to the relational may empty education of its moral and social purpose. Not only does failure to attend to the *relational* [emphasis added] threaten the values expressed in educational (as opposed to anti- or non-educational) practices, but it threatens agency and solidarity among participants in those practices. In our view, restoring focus on the relational dimensions of education will sustain future educational and societal growth, and provide resources of hope for educators: a sense of cohesion of purpose, commonality of direction (solidarity), and a sense of collective power and control (agency).
> (Edwards-Groves, Brennan Kemmis, Hardy and Ponte, 2010, p. 43)

Middle leaders, because of their positioning *in the middle*, are critical agents for facilitating and nourishing such a culture of relational trust. Their *middleness* enables the distinctive kind of supportive and empathetic leadership critical to transforming professional learning in schools in principled, and ultimately sustainable, ways.

In this next section, we now turn to presenting a substantial discussion of ways a 'dialogic approach' opens up a communicative space for leading professional learning. In this more extensive section, we provide some practical ideas that are well-grounded in educational theory, philosophy and research. It opens up this a question for middle leaders, *how does a dialogic approach relate to middle leading for professional learning in individual school sites*?

Facilitating trust through a dialogic approach to professional learning

Developing new education practices means paying close attention to what is happening in actual sites where education happens (like in the staff meeting room or in the classroom). Practices always happen somewhere; and so, what happens, and has happened, in the site is central to understanding and changing practices. We consider that it is the dialogues that take place in professional learning that recognises the critical position 'the site' – the *where*, has for facilitating development. Dialogue creates a common ground upon which new practices can be understood and developed, so in this chapter we highlight the value of a dialogic approach to designing and negotiating site-based professional learning. By *dialogue*, we do not mean the kind of talk that simply delivers information or administrative routines and expectations to teachers, but rather, it is an approach to professional learning that opens up a shared communicative space, where everyone can have a say, and that maximise teacher engagement in their learning experiences.

Leading with dialogic processes connect the *professional learning space* to the *teaching space*, as new ideas are shared and can then be used in the classroom practices of colleagues. However, this does not just happen – it requires thoughtful planning, and an expectation that dialogues will be robust and dynamic. It is the purpose of this chapter to set down a series of core dialogic principles that inform middle leaders work as they facilitate action-oriented professional learning programmes. These are designed within specific contexts based upon an understanding of their being engaged in a practice that morphs and changes as the conditions in the professional practice, themselves, continue to evolve in response to the needs and desires of the teachers and students involved.

Grounding professional learning in the site: shifting practice towards dialogic learning

They know what they know – they bring what they bring

People come to professional learning for a range of reasons, with a range of knowledges, experiences, and expectations, with a range of beliefs and theories, and from a range of communities and circumstances. Each of these factors form the conditions which the middle leader, in leading professional learning, must respond. These also are valuable resources upon which the middle leader can, and should, capitalise. With this in mind, part of the role of the middle leader is to create practice architectures that move teachers *to turn a mirror to themselves* (Edwards-Groves and Davidson, 2017) to support teachers recognise what they know. To do this means designing opportunities that provide conditions (practice architectures) for teachers to better understand themselves and their practices in order to form, reform, and transform their teaching practices.

In reality, for teacher self-awareness and development to happen it has to work in ways that, simultaneously, responds in nuanced ways to the needs and circumstances of their students, but also works strategically with school or system initiatives, agendas or directives. The challenge and complexity for middle leaders is that this position is one that brings with it a responsibility for keeping both of these groups – their needs and agendas – in view. But, bringing others into new or changed practices itself requires responsive nuanced practice – practices that draw on the factors (mentioned above) as fundamental resources for strengthening the foundation from which to build teacher capacity. These practices are animated in and through dialogues.

As an example, middle leader, Hamish, realised the need for a dialogic approach in his school as he considered ways to support the staff in his school more effectively integrate technology into their lessons. Initially in this school, teachers had indicated their interest in integrating technology into their lessons, and had participated in a number of compulsory 'one-off' district PD sessions. However, he noticed that teachers had made little shift in their pedagogical practices. To respond to this, he needed to change the approach; Hamish recognised the need to proceed with a dialogic focus that began with the recognition and identification of what teachers already knew. So, in consultation with the principal and with the support of the district IT consultant, he designed the following 'opt-in plan' for any 'interested' teachers:

1 an introductory situational analysis – with a focus on listening, aimed to gauge the level of teacher comfort, expertise and interest, and to generate teachers' individual professional learning action plans;
2 with the support of the IT consultant, lead a full day professional learning session – this aimed to provide professional input and guided practice (including software demonstrations, guided practice and critique, a focus on what new metalanguage and classroom activities like understanding elements of design for producing multimodal texts in class);
3 at least three two hour in-class sessions with each teacher – this aimed to support individual teachers through co-teaching and/or demonstrations, with follow-up coaching, debrief and mentoring conversations (as negotiated) with the middle leader; and,
4 opportunities for teachers (e.g. for those the less confident) to work more closely with the middle leader for additional in-class sessions (Edwards-Groves, 2012).

Throughout the project, Hamish organised the teachers to meet at least fortnightly to discuss their learning in staff meetings previously held for 'general business'. Hamish arranged for the staff meetings to be handed over to reflective professional dialogues concerning the 'successes and challenges' teachers experienced in student learning in relation to the technology practices that they were trialling in their own lessons. He soon noticed that the 'opt-in' approach generated a 'snowball' effect where more and more teachers joined the conversation becoming committed to the project.

As this *story from practice* shows, reflective practitioners engage in focused professional discussions with others (including their students) about their practices, learning and discoveries. Over time, as teachers – in the company of others, think critically and analytically about their knowledge and teaching practices, and discuss what they have discovered and seen work with their students. These dialogic processes generate possibilities for collaborative learning as teachers soon realise that their views, assumptions and knowledge have progressed – they have learnt (Glenn, 2004). Such pedagogically-focused conversations support teachers in the development of their ability to describe classroom practices (their actions and interactions), and perhaps, to write about their teaching in a focused and critically analytic way so they can interpret and learn from their own teaching. Teachers, then, develop the capacity to change practice because it is based on and informed by evidence about their own realities (Edwards-Groves, 2003).

Importantly, dialogic learning is responsive, because it both creates and, at the same time, is created, by a space for talk and interaction, with a focus on learning and collaboratively working on solutions to shared issues and challenges. Furthermore, it is importantly also about taking a shared responsibility for making it work. Open communicative spaces – and the dialogic professional learning they foster, develops in three inextricably connected realms[1] as middle leaders, teachers and principals:

i   use language and discourses (their *sayings*) that create a shared *semantic space* where they seek to understand one another through communication and intersubjective meaning making;
ii   engage in activities (individually and collectively) using material resources and interacting with one another to say and do things (their *doings*) in *physical space time* in 'real' time meetings, sessions and professional learning activities and tasks; and
iii relate to one another in interactions that develop and nourish interpersonal relationships (their *relatings*) that both create and are created by a *social space* that shares and uses collective power to build capacity, solidarity and trusting relationships.

In practices, these three realms are interdependent and always ever present (to varying degrees of course), but it is the dialogue that is the thread that binds them together in communicative space. So, in doing professional learning together, people come to understand one another, their practices, and the conditions that influence their practices. Thus, the middle leader's role is to open and sustain a dialogic learning space facilitated by shared language, shared activity, and their relationships with the other teacher participants.

Opening the communicative space – building a foundation for trust in professional learning

A hallmark of an *open, trusting,* and *democratic* communicative space is its dialogic approach to professional learning. This is coupled with the aim of deepening teacher's understandings about their practices as they think about, discuss and evaluate meanings taken from the professional discussions, resources and activities they engage with. What teachers understand, how they come to these understandings, and how they justify them are evident in what they say and do (that is, in their practices), and these provide insights into teachers' thinking, their knowledge and reasoning, and also provides opportunities for uncovering misunderstandings and misconceptions. In other words, what teachers think, know and believe is important because it is outworked in practice! Thus, a central part of middle leading is to create a shared space, where teachers are engaged in shared meaning making, as this is the cornerstone for the professional learning. To do this requires 'getting on the same page' by creating an open and dialogic space which supports:

- inclusivity and access for all;
- generative thinking and robust discussion about ideas;
- substantive dialogue about the details of the topic at hand;
- teacher engagement and agency;
- knowledge and understandings through reasoning and evidence-informed talk; and
- shared responsibility for developing, displaying and sustaining the:
  - professional learning community,
  - substantive reasoning that drives highly intellectual, practice-oriented conversations, and
  - knowledge that is secure and grounded deeply in the site.

(adapted from Edwards-Groves, Anstey and Bull, 2014)

These are principles for creating and opening up communicative spaces for developing *practice communities* and for *building relational trust* necessary for site-based professional learning. As such, dialogic learning also *deprivatises practice* (Kemmis, Wilkinson *et al.*, 2014). Noting that communities of practice do not simply appear by virtue of circumstance, they need to be built and nourished over time in a highly principled way. In the *story from practice* below, Joyanne ties building a community ripe for professional learning, to the need for first establishing a foundation based on strong democratic principles, and that in her experience this requires time, persistence, openness, and humility. To illustrate these ideas, we now outline another *story from practice* from an Early Years context.

Stories from practice: building community through democratising professional learning

With the Early Years teaching team comprising six teachers in her school, middle leader and Year 2 teacher Joyanne was initiating an action research project that focused on the development of student's vocabulary in writing. Because of Joyanne's previous experience as a literacy coach prior to coming to the school, she was asked by the principal (who was concerned about the national test results for writing) to take responsibility for leading the initiative. For Joyanne, experience told her that the most challenging part was establishing a climate for open and honest professional dialogue where teachers were confident and comfortable to contribute by '*making their practice public*' and '*opening up*' to '*disclose the messiness of changing*' to '*divulge their uncertainties to peers*'. She explains further:

> The first thing is that it takes time, genuine time, sometimes longer than you expect, but it is worth the investment for sure. I have been to so many PDs where the terms 'professional learning communities' and 'communities of practice' come up, but no one really moves from these as cliched or aspirational descriptions of collaborative teacher development. I know from experience that these just don't happen overnight; you need time, openness and trust, and communication. These are the keys to developing and building a learning community where everyone feels accepted and in control...
>
> The second thing is, I have to really put myself out there too, to get teachers talking openly and honestly. I have to be open about my own challenges with my Year 2s, but discipline myself to not control, not overpower the conversation by telling them what I thought all the time, even though sometimes that's what is needed. Holding back is hard, and still I have to keep practising that part so everyone has the chance to share, feel included, and believe their own experiences are valued. It's not neat, it's sometimes very messy. But, to me, its success hinges on the dialogue and commitment to it; it makes a huge difference to how things progress, but in the end the right way to go.

Joyanne's sentiments identify the centrality of a socially just, deprivatised and democratic space for establishing the fundamental platform from which a community can legitimately grow and develop. It also shows her solidarity with her teaching colleagues. Her comments reflect the need for legitimacy, freedom, and shared power, and show how these ideas are tangled up with one another in the *messiness* and complexity of practice. A dialogic space is one that enables discussion and deliberation; it is an iterative space for *dialogue that feeds community that feeds democratic ways of working.* The six principles of dialogue are explored in more detail next.

i. Building inclusivity

To be truly dialogic means opening the communicative space where everyone is treated equally and accorded dignity and respect, thus involving everyone concerned. To this end, the teachers and middle leader need to have a shared understanding, and dedicated time for focused professional discussions. This creates the *dynamic* and arrangements characteristic of open dialogic practices. This also affords an inclusive community that is necessary for addressing the kinds of challenging concepts, confusions, misconceptions, or not well-developed ideas that often arise in professional learning. Inclusive spaces make it possible for discussion and deliberation and disagreement, complex and problematic ideas and thoughts to be treated as important, interesting, and opportunities to learn more. Through scaffolding and facilitator support (from the middle leader), a climate of inclusivity emerges as teacher participants share meanings, collaborate in accomplishing activities, and relate in ways which establish demonstrate genuine trusting relationships (discussed in more detail in the next section).

ii. Building capacity for generative thinking and robust discussion

To build the capacity for leading and employing generative thinking and robust discussion among teachers, middle leaders need to make deliberate moves to shift closed and narrow talk towards an open dialogic space. Such a move provides teachers the time and opportunity for thinking and discussing in productive and vigorous ways; thus, expanding teacher's repertoire or capacities for engaging critically with each other's ideas. Put simply, if teachers have more quality time and opportunity for talk about genuine 'on topic' ideas then they are developing shared understandings by practising articulating and sharing meanings; and if they are practising, they are developing knowledge and building capacity for their pedagogical practices.

iii. Building substantive dialogue

A dialogic approach enables teachers to engage deeply in talk with substance. Building substantive dialogue requires talking about things that matter to the learning purposes, and teasing out what is known and needs to be known about the topic on hand. It requires uncovering where these ideas, theories and issues came from, and in what ways do they relate to current needs and circumstances? What is missing or needed? What is relevant here? In other words, to engage in substantive dialogue requires explicit thought and discussion about how the current practices emerged, and their *connectedness* to what has been common practice, and why it has become sedimented in the particular site. It makes links to and builds on prior knowledge and experiences. For example, physical education teachers might ask why they require all students partake in swimming carnivals; senior primary school teachers might ask why they still teach long-division; early years teachers might ponder the use of phonics and/or whole language approaches to reading. As this learning focused talk is co-constructed through dialogue, teachers learn to expand their own repertoires by 'digging deeper', 'building on', and engaging actively with each other's ideas, as they:

- listen to one another;
- think about what they are hearing to deepen the focus of their own thinking, understandings, and reasoning;
- give others time to think;
- respond with and engage with the reasoning and ideas of others;
- respect alternative viewpoints; and
- come to consensus where necessary.

iv. Building teacher agency

Dialogic approaches shift the power balance because, in an open communicative space, there is a sense of agency, consensual decision making, and shared power. This means that teachers as genuine participants have the capacity for shaping their own knowledge, skills and values. As professionals, it repositions teachers with the agency to be involved in shaping both their learning and the learning agenda. Therefore, in a dialogic space, the middle leader's practices must aim to engender teacher *agency* so they can be agentic professionals who shape and direct their own learning and development. As suggested by Kemmis *et al.* (2014):

> There is a tendency in our times to imagine that processes like education and schooling are technical processes concerned with the production of things – the production of people of a certain kind, for example, or the production of 'learning outcomes'.
>
> (p. 25)

This is a technical view that considers what we do in education as mainly dispensary – transactional from the *top down*, primarily overlooks the professional agency of the teacher who is responsible for what they learn or do not learn, and for their own self-formation. Rather, a dialogic approach entrusts the teachers with their learning by positioning them as co-constructors of their development. Through evidence-informed dialogues, they have the power to initiate action, to agree and disagree, to extend and challenge the ideas of others and make justifiable claims for example. And so, knowledge, skills and values are constructed by the professional agency and activity of the teacher, in concert and collaboration with others.

v. Building knowledge and understandings through reasoning and evidence

To build knowledge, dialogues need to be evidence-informed. Dialogue connects knowledge to evidence. Therefore, evidence-informed dialogues begin with what is known; the knowledge or information gathered or developed from a range of evidentiary sources (for example, experiences, work samples, assessment information, texts, lessons transcripts, reflections, websites, or other public information). Through the use of dialogue, teachers and middle leaders marshal the evidence into coherent ideas or arguments, because they are aware that all claims require justification and evidence. By creating opportunities for teachers to make logical connections between what they know, what they have experienced, what they think, and what they have heard or read, they can build reasoned understandings. It is not simply about building a foundation, but about building deep knowledge from a strong evidence base. This often involves searching for premises – including questioning or challenging the premises of others' claims, rather than simply supporting or refuting conclusions.

Here, the middle leader scaffolds teachers towards talking more 'academically' about concepts in order to make productive attempts at sense making. Teachers can then be supported to build logical arguments; come to consensus based on evidence; develop rationales; make claims and justify them; analyse the claims of others; and recognise incomplete, undeveloped, or even incorrect claims or half formed ideas. Dialogic approaches, furthermore, encourage participants to use subject specific metalanguage in their theorising as they share their ideas, opinions, and knowledge.

i. Building shared responsibility

Professional learning built on dialogic principles builds a strong sense of shared responsibility on three levels:

1. *Responsibility to the professional learning community* – It is talk in which all participating teachers have an equal and shared responsibility to respectfully 'go public with their thinking' and to be demonstrably listening. They share their thinking, ideas, and opinions. They listen to and build their contributions in response to those of others and ask each other questions aimed at clarifying or expanding a proposition. In this, teachers, acting not alone but collectively and with agency, have responsibility for their part in the conduct of the practice to initiate and sustain action-oriented professional learning. 'I think that…'; 'I heard you say…'; 'My opinion is…'; 'What do you think…'; 'It's your turn…'.
2. *Responsibility to substantive reasoning* – It is talk where teachers take responsibility for elaborating on and explaining more about the topic or concept. In this, teachers regulate their learning, share in making meaning, make logical connections between the ideas, and draw logical conclusions using

evidence and rationalisation. 'I think this because ...'; 'Why did you think ...?'; 'What did you mean by...?'; 'I disagree because...'.
3 *Responsibility for developing, displaying, and securing knowledge* – It is each teacher participant's responsibility to make attempts to get their facts right and to provide the evidence behind their ideas, opinions, or claims. They also have the responsibility to challenge each other when the evidence is lacking or unavailable. 'I know ...'; 'I read this ...'; 'that contradicts with...'; 'Can you clarify ...'.

The particular conditions described in the section – inclusivity, capacity building, substantive dialogue, teacher agency, developing knowledge and understandings, responsibility – are created through the ways professional learning conversations are organised and enacted whatever kinds of professional learning is on offer, and where each person's contributions are treated as a resource for learning more.

Dialogic practice as producing conditions for communicating

Taking the conditions for a dialogic approach into action requires creating conditions in which the sayings (language), doings (actions, activities and tasks), and ways of relating (relationships) are formed around five complementary principles (adapted from Alexander, 2006, p. 28, 37–43). To support the professional learning to be dialogic, middle leaders should move the conversations to be:

1 *collective* – where middle leaders address professional learning tasks together with teachers as a shared responsibility for learning and collaborative co-production;
2 *reciprocal* – where participants listen to each other, share ideas, and consider alternative viewpoints;
3 *cumulative* – where participants build on each other's contributions and chain them into coherent lines of thinking bringing cohesion across lines of ideas, opinions and concepts which otherwise might remain fragmented and implicit; this forms a 'double loop' as the talk connects back and forth, between and across participants and topics;
4 *supportive and inclusive* – where participants help each other to reach common understandings; support one another to develop, display, and secure knowledge; each has agency to express their ideas, opinions and understandings of concepts freely and without fear of embarrassment over 'wrong' answers;
5 *purposeful and explicit* – where the professional talk, though open and dialogic, is also planned and structured with specific professional learning goals kept in view and these are expressed with clarity and sustained throughout the session from introduction to review. The middle leader does not leave learning to chance, and ensures learning has taken place.

Enacting principled dialogues form strong foundations for democracy and inclusivity that at the same time form conditions for building knowledge and relationships. How these eventuate, or indeed are arranged, in the 'real time' flow influences the substantive learning and learning practices participants encounter (Kemmis et al., 2014).

Professional learning conversations through dialogic practice

As leaders or even teachers, we often underestimate the power of our dialogic practices. This section considers talk and interaction practices in professional learning – how they are organised and what they accomplish. In the earlier section of this chapter we provided a lot of ideas that can help middle leaders understand and conduct a democratic dialogic professional learning space, and so now we want to look at what this might look like *in practice*. Therefore, here we aim to assist middle leaders to learn more about ways that dialogic learning operates in a professional educational setting. Dialogic learning makes it possible for teachers to be open to learning through communicative practices which give form and substance to collaborative meaning making. Widening the approach calls for deliberate, open, and explicit *dialogic practices* (talk moves) that are interactive, and responsive to local needs and conditions. These *dialogic practices* are strategic and planned moves which build capacity through opening up a communicative space for professional learning by enabling participants to:

1 sustain the focal point
2 extend and deepen thinking
3 challenge thinking
4 demonstrate active listening
5 allow wait time for thinking and formulating
6 ask open guiding questions
7 withhold your own point of view
8 give learning focused responses
9 reflect on, respond to, and review learning.

In professional learning conversations, like those that form part of study circles or professional dialogue conferences, these *dialogic talk moves* are not mutually exclusive and often occur as overlapping and intertwined. Drawing on these interactive *dialogic talk moves* in strategic ways enables the middle leader, as a facilitator of the professional learning, to create an open dialogic culture for teacher participants to deepen reasonings, develop knowledge, understand their experiences and expectations, identify beliefs and theories, and become fully responsive to their student's communities and circumstances. Each of these practices (adapted from Edwards-Groves, Anstey and Bull, 2014) will be described next to provide practical examples to assist middle leaders facilitate a dialogic approach to professional learning.

1 Sustaining the focal point

This dialogic practice invites individual participants to offer a range of responses to a question or challenge and affords them an extended talk time to deepen their thinking; they have the opportunity to share and then explore their own ideas further and to build onto or elaborate *their own line of thought*. In this approach, particular probes or provocations are used which 'press for reasoning' (Michaels and O'Connor, 2015) and provides the time for teachers to demonstrate a substantive engagement with the topic. This invites teachers to sustain their thinking about an idea, concept, or opinion as they share 'more complete' ideas, then extend, elaborate, and clarify their own thinking and responses. What results is the chance for teachers to offer more coherent and cogent ideas or opinions and to extend these further by providing evidence to support their points or claims.

In professional learning, the place of evidentiary talk makes what is said accountable to all present in the learning community, to substantive reasoning as teachers show their understandings in their responses and to the content knowledge being taken up and explored in the session. Here, participants develop responsibility for their part in the professional learning of the community, for substantiating reasoning and for seeking out and expressing what is known in relation to the facts, known experiences, or evidence. In this practice the middle leader facilitates dialogue through productive questioning (using open-ended, critical, and inferential questions). These invite teachers to extend, elaborate on and deepen their own ideas before the floor is opened to the rest of the group.

> Some examples:
> What else do you know about this topic Albert?
> How does the idea connect to other books/articles we have read, or what Annette said previously?
> How do the ideas connect to another topic we have covered before? Go further Mikael?
> Could you tell us a little bit more about that idea?
> Tell us why you've chosen to do it that way, Otto.
> Why do you think that Mikaela?
> What's your evidence, Isabel?
> How did you arrive at that conclusion?
> Is there anything in the text that made you think that?
> What makes you say that?
> Tell me why you think that way. Why?
> Can you say more about that? What do you mean by that?
> Can you give an example from your own experience?
> Can you provide some evidence to support your point of view?

> Can you elaborate on that point a little more?
> How do you know that?
> Where did you get that idea from?
> What are the implications of your response?

2 Extending and deepening thinking

This dialogic practice means opening up the floor to other members of the group – as a community of learners – to explore ideas, opinions, and concepts more deeply. The middle leader uses probing questions which provoke teacher participants to extend the thinking of others. In this, teachers are asked to elaborate or add on to the ideas and propositions of others, provide more depth and detail, provide more evidence to endorse the knowledge or facts being presented, and to substantiate thoughts, claims and opinions or to clarify the responses of others.

This kind of professional talk produces evidentiary talk that builds a foundation for developing knowledge and deepening reasoning, especially when exploring complex ideas or difficult concepts. The extending move enables teachers to identify and build on *half formed* ideas, as the middle leader presses them for reasoning to substantiate points. It activates the principle for taking shared responsibility for the professional learning.

> Some examples:
> Who can tell me more about that idea? proposition? concept?
> Now dig deep, what else can you add to Dani's point?
> Who can add onto the idea that Jake is building?
> Can anyone take that suggestion and push it a little further?
> Anyone else want to add to Tilly's idea?
> Why do you think Ange came to that conclusion?
> Who can add some evidence?
> Is there anything from the text we read that you can add?
> Tell me why you think that way. Why?
> Can you say more about that? What do you mean by that?
> Who can give another example?
> Where else can you find out?
> What are the implications of Mike's response?

3 Challenging thinking

This dialogic practice addresses the need for teachers as learners to develop reasoning skills and professional capacities for building opinion, argument, debate, viewpoints, questioning, judgement, discussion, persuasion, and

68 *Relating, trust, and dialogic practice*

exposition. It also lays a path for developing broad consciousness by assisting participants to uncover and challenge bias, stereotypes, and misconceptions.

Using provocations, like those exemplified below, middle leaders can scaffold teachers to not simply justify their own responses, but to assist them to respond to and build arguments, offer counter arguments, pose questions, and to challenge the thinking or reasoning of others. Probes and provocations which challenge thinking assist to develop logical thinking and capacities for persuasion and argumentation; questions for further investigation may be raised.

> Some examples:
> Would anyone like to respond to that idea?
> Would what Ivy said, apply in all circumstances?
> Does anyone have a different opinion?
> How else could we view this?
> *As a challenge or counter example*: Does it always work that way?
> How does that idea square with Alfie's example?
> How consistent is this response with what others might be thinking?
> How might we be able to combine both the ideas of Edric and Gretel?
> What if it had been this instead?
> Do you agree/disagree Jen? (And why?)
> Are you saying the same thing as Angus or something different, and if it's different, how is it different?
> What do people think about what Haddie said?
> Does anyone want to respond to that idea?

4 Demonstrating active listening

Through reconceptualising or reframing a response, this dialogic practice aims to clarify meaning (always checking that the person is comfortable with the reframing) through revoicing. Revoicing leaves open the opportunity for a speaker to respond again so that they may clarify their thought or extend it even further. Each contribution is treated as a resource for development and further thinking as the teachers engage with each other's contributions. The newly reframed contribution of the talk displays – as members of the conversation revoice, repeat, or reframe the contribution – that they have listened to and considered the ideas, opinions, or the facts-in-evidence of others.

It is an interactive move which demands interdependency in professional learning as, for example, the person repeats or reformulates a previous contribution, in an attempt to clarify, or recast (rephrase and/or reframe) the response for the entire group, or compare it to someone else's contribution. This shows genuine engagement with the topic and can assist scaffolding and developing the discussion points further.

Some examples:
    Do you know what I heard you doing/saying just then? –
    You may not have realised it, but your point agrees with Thomas, who suggested...
    In summary, you are saying....
    So Jena you're saying that.........?
    So, let me see if I've got what you're saying Jessi. Are you saying.? (always leaving space for the original contributor to agree or disagree and say more)
    You said... is that what you mean?
    Okay, let me see what you are saying...
    So you are saying ...
    Okay – so let me see if I've got your theory right. You're saying that...?
    Right, so your idea is to...
    Can someone summarise what has been said?
    Who can explain what Madeline means when she says that....?
    Who thinks they could explain in their own words why Robert came up with that answer?
    Why do you think he said that?
    Repeating:
    Who can say that again?
    Who can repeat what Jessica just said or put it into their own words?
    After 'Partner Talk' – what did your partner say?

5 Allowing wait time for thinking and formulating

This practice is well known among teachers, yet it is the reality that it is not often practised effectively (as teachers and middle leaders are sometimes uncomfortable with silence) – especially in professional learning activities. The purpose of 'wait time' is to give members of the group enough time to make/construct/formulate a response they are comfortable with before they 'go public' with their response 'out loud'. It is an inclusive practice as it doesn't put participants on the spot to respond quickly; they have enough time to think through their ideas, to craft and rehearse responses (and provides valuable time that can preserve a person's dignity). In addition, it is a dialogic practice where sufficient space is provided in both the conversation *and* in the formulating activities (for instance through partner talk or writing things down which also provides thinking time). For this reason, it is strategic to also consider what other interactive or reflection activities to put in place to enable focused thinking (see Appendix 1 for other helpful examples).

Ultimately, if we are to be truly responsive, it is important for the middle leader to provide enough wait time for thinking and formulating after posing a question, after calling on a person to answer, or after a person gives a response.

> Some examples:
> This is a complex question, so we need to allow some extra thinking time.
> Take your time with this Tina. We'll wait...
> Hold on. Let Kirsten finish her thought.
> It's okay Tess, we'll wait for you to collect your thoughts...
> Now that was an interesting idea Jonno, let's think about that some more.

6 Ask open guiding questions

In one respect questioning, although taken for granted, is a practice which requires explicit thought and preparation. Asking more open questions is a talk move which invites dialogue and aims to guide those involved in the conversation into deeper levels of focus and cohesion. The practice is based on the premise 'good questions yield good responses'. Choosing the right question can lead teachers to higher, more meaningful understandings of their practices.

A *guiding question* is one which *opens* up the professional learning space by providing a fundamental query that is directed towards developing understanding, and:

- embracing *in-depth thinking* and encourages scope for *multiple viewpoints*;
- turning topics into questions opens up the floor for a range of perspectives to emerge;
- provoking teachers to think deeply about the range of possibilities and issues;
- enabling critical reasoning as ideas are substantiated and justified;
- allowing for flexibility in responses, investigation methods, and presentation modes;
- providing space for substantive (real, authentic, in-depth) conversation; and
- engaging with topics with a higher degree of intellectual focus.

> Some examples:
> What makes a sustainable practice?
> What makes a good mathematics programme?
> What makes an inquiry project?
> What makes a balanced reading programme?
> What makes good assessment?
> What makes this a useful strategy for supporting comprehension?
> What makes a good coach? Facilitator? mentor?
> What makes an effective lesson?
> What makes a good teacher? Learner?
> What makes a good resource?
> Why is assessment useful to the student learning? When? How?
> *Why* questions are the essence of inquiry, why?

7 Withholding your point of view: vacating the floor

In this dialogic talk move, the middle leader refrains from controlling the 'conversational floor'. They exercise restraint by withholding their turn and holding back from initiating a dialogue that begins with their own opinions or ideas. Its aim is to legitimate teachers' contributions by reserving their personal control of the dialogue; they do this by handing the control to the learners through withholding or suspending their own comment to allow the conversation to progress without them dominating. To assist the process, the middle leader may reconfigure the physical arrangements so that the teachers in the physical space are enabled to speak out in the discussion. Here participants are handed more control of the dialogue enabling a more democratic space where:

a   all participants have opportunities to contribute;
b   teachers are in pairs or small groups to think about, develop, rehearse and/ or test ideas before they are made public in a larger forum (the whole group);
c   time is added for more opportunities for teachers to listen to and respond to each other's ideas in a smaller, more intimate forum;
d   responsibilities are dispersed, managed and shared among participants. They take more ownership and exercise agency as the arrangements are changed to equalise the power balance between the middle leader and the teachers; and
e   there are opportunities for different leading roles across the development process.

Appendix 2 provides some useful examples to orchestrate vacating the floor. It is important to note, however, that one role of the middle leader is ensure the floor is distributed between those present so that one person or a few people do not dominate the conversation.

8 Giving learning focused responses

Providing learning focused responses is a constructive, considered and non-judgemental talk move. It is a dialogic practice used when the middle leader wants to clarify and extend what the teacher means in an unthreatening way. To do this, middle leaders can reflect back the responses (through revoicing or repeating) and further explicate how the teacher might have come to the particular response or answer. Responses remain focused on both deepening thinking about the topic, and on building knowledge through the dialogue. It often finds its form in feedback, but feedback has no effect in a vacuum – it needs to be evidence-informed and context related.

72 Relating, trust, and dialogic practice

Responding here is related to feedback, and negotiating the *feedup-feedback-feedforward* loop forms an important part of middle leading. Butler and Winne (1995) claimed that 'feedback is information with which a learner can confirm, add to, overwrite, tune, or restructure information in memory, whether that information is domain knowledge, meta-cognitive knowledge, beliefs about self and tasks, or cognitive tactics and strategies' (p. 5740). To be powerful in its effect, there must be a learning context to which the response or the feedback is addressed. And ultimately, feedback needs to be used in ways that specifically contribute to teacher development and student learning and improvement.

Feedback is but part of the professional learning process and is most powerful when it addresses *misinterpretations*, not a total lack of understanding. It is an interactive communicative talk move that provides an opportunity for the middle leader to address issues of 'reasoning' as he/she makes an attempt to *tease out* and clarify any points of confusion, misinformation or tension. Dealing with errors, confusions, misconceptions, or half-formed ideas are important opportunities to learn more, rather than 'issues' being brushed over or ignored. Selecting the right words is crucial; participants know that 'mmm' is not a helpful comment; neither is a direct reallocation of their response to another 'more knowledgeable person' for example. Similarly, effusive praise can be equally problematic. While teachers might need to be affirmed, effusive praise can stifle risk taking and disrupt the dialogue, so minimising effusive feedback is often an important way to strategically to maintain the flow of ideas coming out in the dialogue. In this, the participants are given the opportunity to reconsider or refine their responses.

> Some examples:
> Do you know what I heard you doing/saying just then? –
> You're on the right track; let's think about this some more.
> You may not have realised it, but you …
> Where are you going with this?
> How are you going with that?
> Where to next?
> Minimising feedback:
> Thank you for that idea, have you got more to add.
> That's an interesting perspective, what else …
> Yes that's one way, what others …

9 Reflecting, responding to, and reviewing learning: the 3Rs for dialogic learning

> If we don't reflect, we are teaching 'in the dark' without knowing if we are being effective and if we should modify our teaching …
>
> (Friel, 1997)

All teachers reflect on, or think about, their lessons from time-to-time, but for the most part this is often where it ends. It is often ad hoc and superficial with little or no impact on practice development or student learning. *Reflection, response, and review* are dialogic practices that establish a critical and analytic stance towards learning and engaging with topics more deeply. *Reflection* sits alongside *response* and *review* as a tool for learning: together these three practices form the '3Rs'. Merely thinking about teaching is not enough to effect practice. The proposition here is that reflection needs to be learned, practiced, and actioned. Further, without focus or action (demonstrating an active response or change of direction or approach), reflection is not constructive. There are two dimensions to this professional learning practice to be considered:

1   reflecting on, reviewing, and responding to learning processes (how);
2   reflecting on, reviewing, and responding to substantive learning (what).

To *step out of the dark* to develop a deep awareness about their own teaching, teachers need to be supported to question their effectiveness and whether or not modifications to their practices are necessary or effective. Stopping to think about, write about, respond to, question, and test one's assumptions, actions and experiences, and to take other points of view into consideration, are reflective responsive experiences pivotal in teaching and professional learning. But these are not activities that 'just happen' (Dillon, 2002), or come naturally. Instead they need to be planned for and learnt (and taught). For teachers, reflection must assist in the construction, consolidation and expression of their professional knowledge and practice. For middle leaders, it must be focused on teacher learning and followed with purposeful responsive action in classrooms with students. It also needs to extend teacher understandings (about themselves and their students) and affect a change in practice. Assisting teachers to think about details of their practice, in particular their classroom interactions, is a feature of effective professional development and a responsibility of educational systems.

Part of the role of the middle leader is to take teachers to a deeper level of thinking – one that injects challenge and promotes focused thought on very specific aspects of practice, beliefs, and student learning. This is necessary because 'it is not possible for teachers to change their teaching practices if those practices are not made the object of thought and consideration' (Hart, 1992). To be action-oriented and responsive teachers need to set aside time and be given opportunities to reflect on, review, respond to, and to ask questions routinely and deliberately about their teaching, and use the answers to challenge, guide, and change their teaching practices in a highly focused way. Then, as truly reflective practitioners, they can respond constructively by acting on what they discover.

74 Relating, trust, and dialogic practice

Practices to support reflection, response and review

Focused reflection, response, and review can be supported by critically selecting appropriate strategies suitable for the teachers and their specific context so these become routinely embedded within thought and action (see Appendix 1 and 3). To inform reflection and stimulate problem-solving and decision-making conversations, evidence is an interface to the classroom that can be gathered systematically through a range of techniques. For example:

- *Audio-video recording lessons:* Focused review of teaching on video, in transcripts or listening to recordings of lessons enables teachers to stop time, to step back to look more closely at the details of their practice in a clear and critically analytic way.
- *Written logs:* Journals enable teachers to record personal accounts on a regular basis and to gather thoughts on paper as they relate to their classroom experiences; these are useful for documenting details, interpretations, explanations, hypotheses, feelings and reflections about lesson observations; these can facilitate personal professional growth and focused change.
- *Peer observation and debrief:* Focused observation, review and peer debriefing strengthens thinking about teachers' own teaching. Talking about teaching with middle leaders as 'critical friends' helps teachers discover key issues or trends about their own teaching.
- *Pictorial records:* in the form of concepts maps, mind maps, photographs, drawings of floor plans etc form useful supplements to stimulate recall of events in practice.
- *Teach and look back:* Regular time taken to ask predetermined questions focusing on lesson details (see Appendix 3 for a guide), targets thinking toward the effectiveness of teachers' own work whilst constructing and extending knowledge about teaching. Others might include: What did you notice? What went well? What surprised you? What challenged you?

Conclusion

Dialogic professional learning supports practices which leverage action-oriented professional learning partnerships between teachers by creating:

i an open semantic space for supporting the development of apposite discourses and developing intersubjective meaning making;

ii an open physical space and time for supporting action and building and scaffolding; and
iii an open social space for developing strong relational trust and culture of learning among teachers.

For the middle leader, who negotiates and facilitates programmes of professional learning with teachers, dialogic participation creates conditions for relational trust that move teacher's thinking from surface level to deeper level thinking – from ideas to embodied enacted practices. This chapter showed ways that dialogic professional learning forms a responsive, participatory, and dynamic space that facilitates active learning and participation in discussions about complex and often challenging educational issues. On occasions, this may mean supporting colleagues to grasp a new or challenging concept, to adjust familiar practices, or to learn new a skill or way of teaching. Drawing on the principles described in the chapter, professional dialogues generate formative discussions that require using deliberative and critical reasoning processes to maximise uptake and possibilities for development. Dialogic professional learning lays the groundwork for building strong interpersonal relationships and relational trust that produces necessary conditions for affirmative professional action, teacher agency, and accomplishing change.

Theory-into-practice (TIPs): questions for reflection and discussion

1 In your role as a middle leader, how can you see a dialogic approach to professional learning working in your site? What may be the conditions that constrain the possibilities for deep and meaningful dialogue?
2 Consider how each of the six dialogic principles democratise professional learning (by building inclusivity, capacity for generative thinking and robust discussion, substantive dialogue, teacher agency, and knowledge and understandings through reasoning and evidence), create an open communicative space in your setting.
3 Do they align with your beliefs and your practices? Discuss.
4 Practise some of the dialogic practices described in the chapter (use the stems provided to support your development).
5 One of the practical dialogic *talk moves* was to 'vacate the floor'. How would you feel about leading from 'behind' and allowing others to have a major role in the professional discussion?

Note

1 This draws on the ideas from the theory of practice architectures outlined in Chapter 2.

References

Alexander, R. (2006). *Towards Dialogic Teaching: rethinking classroom talk*, 2nd edition. York: Dialogos.

Butler, D. and Winne, P. (1995). 'Feedback and Self-Regulated Learning: A Theoretical Synthesis', *Review of Educational Research*, 65(3), 245–281. doi:10.3102/00346543065003245.

Dillon, D. (2002). *Kids Insight: Reconsidering How to Meet the Literacy Needs of All Students*. Newark, DE: International Reading Association.

Edwards-Groves, C. (2003). *On Task: Focused Literacy Learning*. Newtown, Sydney, NSW: Primary English Teaching Association Australia.

Edwards-Groves, C. (2012). 'Interactive creative technologies: Changing learning practices and pedagogies in the writing classroom', *Australian Journal of Language and Literacy*, 35(1), 99–114.

Edwards-Groves, C. and Davidson, C. (2017). *Becoming a Meaning Maker: Talk and Interaction in the Dialogic Classroom*. Newtown, Sydney, NSW: Primary English Teaching Association Australia.

Edwards-Groves, C., Anstey, M. and Bull, G. (2014). *Classroom Talk: Understanding dialogue, pedagogy and practice*. Newtown, Sydney, NSW: Primary English Teaching Association Australia.

Edwards-Groves, C., Grootenboer, P. and Rönnerman, K. (2016). 'Facilitating a culture of relational trust in school-based action research: Recognising the role of middle leaders', *Educational Action Research*, 24(3), 369–386.

Edwards-Groves, C., Brennan Kemmis, R., Hardy, I. and Ponte, P. (2010). 'Relational architectures: Recovering solidarity and agency as living practices in education', *Pedagogy, Culture and Society*, 18(1), 43–54.

Friel, S. (Ed.) (1997). 'The Role of Reflection in Teaching: Do You Need to Change Your Teaching Practices?', *Arithmetic Teacher*, September. National Council of Teachers of Mathematics.

Glenn, W. J. (2004). 'Refining through Reflection: Using the Teaching Journal as a Catalyst for change', *Thinking Classroom: An International Journal of Reading, Writing and Critical Reflection*. 5(1), 21–27.

Hart, L. C. (1992). 'Essentials', *AMP Connection*, 2.

Kemmis, S. and Edwards-Groves, C. (2018). *Understanding Education: History, Politics and Practices*. Singapore: Springer.

Kemmis, S., McTaggart, R. and Nixon, R. (2014). *The action research planner. Doing critical participatory action research*. Singapore: Springer.

Kemmis, S., Wilkinson, J., Edwards-Groves, C., Hardy, I., Grootenboer, P. and Bristol, L. (2014). *Changing Practices, Changing Education*. Singapore: Springer Education.

Michaels, S. and O'Connor, C. (2015). Conceptualizing Talk Moves as Tools: Professional Development Approaches for Academically Productive Discussions. In *Socializing Intelligence Through Academic Talk and Dialogue* (pp. 347–362). Washington, DC: American Educational Research Association. doi:10.3102/978-0-935302-43-1_27.

Further reading

Edwards-Groves, C. (2014). 'Talk Moves: A repertoire of practices for productive classroom dialogue' PETAA PAPER 195. Newtown, Sydney: Primary English Teaching Association Australia.

5 Evidence-informed development

Middle leading and the changing world of teachers' work requires professional learning that, from the outset, supports teachers to understand, gather, and analyse evidence about teaching and student learning – their performance and achievement. This chapter acknowledges the challenges these two aspects of educational work brings to the daily activity of teachers and to the middle leaders that support their development in schools. Associated with this, is the ways in which 'data', 'evidence', and 'best practice' are constructs that require careful interrogation. Middle leading requires considering the matter of what constitutes educational 'evidence' as being directly relevant to the daily practices and improvement of teachers in schools. This is necessary in a climate where the connotations of the term *evidence* continue to bedevil those charged with determining policies and programmes designed to facilitate teacher professional learning.

Supporting teachers to understand, gather, and analyse evidence

In this section, we redraw some boundaries between familiar notions of data and evidence as they are currently positioned in the contemporary educational development landscape. We frame practice development in relation to the idea of *evidence-informed change*. For us, middle leaders need to begin with understanding the relationship between data and evidence and their place in organising, driving, and sustaining their site-based change. Increasingly school leaders and teachers are being asked to collect and respond to *data* about their students' learning and performance. This means that the way data is collected, the nature of the data, and the ways it is analysed and used, are important, and this is often the responsibility of middle leaders. Data can be understood as being highly specific information. To this end, we suggest that middle leaders need to focus more holistically on evidence – and as an analogy, a bit like an environmentalist who has the primary interest and influence on the development of a person or group of persons, who draws on information like an historian (what has happened in the past) as well as an ecologist (what does this mean now for growth and sustainability), rather than solely as a statistician (with a focus on data vis-à-vis student achievement and performance scores).

Therefore, in this chapter we have tended to use the term 'evidence' rather than 'data' – this is not just a semantic exercise, but rather an attempt to convey a broader understanding about how we can know the effects of teaching changes *in* practice. Of course, evidence does include data, but it is an account of data. Since we consider leading professional learning and curriculum development, we consider the need for evidence that helps us to explain trends and practices and to answer questions like: 'What is happening here?'; 'How has this change impacted teaching?'; 'How has this change impacted learning?'; and 'How do we know?'. Crucial here is the point that the primary job of teachers (including middle leaders) is to teach, not to write a major dissertation about their work (although they may want to do this). The main purpose of collecting and analysing evidence is to improve teaching and learning, it needs to be relatively simple, manageable, and considered to be an integral part of teaching. Nonetheless, it is important at the outset to note that the need for evidence is central.

Evidence helps us understand what is happening, not just what we think might be occurring; understanding it ensures development (and the plan for it) is responsive to the actual needs and conditions in classrooms. Evidence allows us to move on from mere hunches or what we think are good ideas, to robust approaches and practices that are well-informed and defensible, as is necessary in any profession (including teaching). This is a view that repositions evidence as being about teaching and learning practices and should inform and guide site-based professional and curriculum development. This sort of information is not about developing a generalised theory or universal answer to a big problem – it is about practitioner enquiry into one's own practices in one's own sites. Kemmis, McTaggart and Nixon (2014) said, in teacher action research:

> we do not aim to produce generalisations about the 'one best way' to do things. In fact, we don't want to find the best way to do things anywhere *except* here – where we are, in our situation.
>
> (p. 69)

From a practice perspective, therefore, the lines between data and evidence must be redrawn in ways that enable practitioners to focus on practices and improvement as they are carried through in their daily activity (and the understanding and development of it).

The relationship between data and evidence: where are we now?

In recent years there has been an increase in demands for teachers, school leaders, systems and even governments to collect data on students' performance and achievement, particularly in 'high stakes' subjects like numeracy and literacy. This is an international phenomenon given precedence through testing regimes like PISA and TIMMS, nationally in Australia through NAPLAN, and then of course locally through standardised assessments like PAT-M and PAT-R and regular school-based tests and assignments. However, the focus on 'data' and its 'effect sizes' seems to have served to narrow our understandings of assessment to that which can be measured and quantified. Amidst this data-driven climate pervading educational practice, we are not convinced that the proliferation of data, and the collection of it, has actually helped to improve the quality of teaching and learning in schools. Rather, as we see it, it has been used as a mechanism to measure and control teachers and schools, if often only for political purposes.

As a response, we outline some practical and manageable ideas about collecting and using evidence to inform teacher's educational development. These ideas, generated through our own research, acknowledge the purpose and place of evidence, which is fundamentally to improve teaching and learning in the site where it unfolds – in classrooms. In other words, ways in which middle leaders and teachers can collect and use their own evidence to enhance their professional practice. In the first half of the chapter we focus gathering evidence in education, and provide some guidelines how these can be used vis-à-vis school-based development. Then we turn to a more detailed use of how transcripts form the evidence that can be critically analysed and used to inform practice development. Throughout the chapter, we provide practical examples from a range of contexts to illustrate what its use might look like in practice.

The matter of evidence in policy, practice and professional change

The matter of what constitutes 'evidence' continues to afflict those charged with determining policies designed to provide for teacher professional learning. A one-time Secretary of State for Education in the UK, Dame Estelle Morris (2011), stated that 'Education is an increasingly evidence-rich policy area. How we use that evidence could determine our future success', arguing that 'quality evidence and the proper use of it are crucial for success in schools'. But what stands as 'evidence-rich policy'? Finding an operational definition outlining the essential nature of evidence is no easy matter whether it is acting as guidance for politicians, educational bureaucrats or those working in the field (Hammersley, 2009). Too often evidence elides into a simplistic 'what works' or 'best practice' discourse, feeding the more instrumental view of practice as that which is a technical exercise. This is a view strongly contested by writers such as Biesta (2010) who sees that a way forward requires an approach that seeks to reduce complexity in circumstances that are anything but simple. This is because, what works *in practice* is always contested, since sites, practices and practitioners are individual, nuanced, and unique. One size does not fit all. At this point, we would rather reframe the question to move from a policy focus to a practice focus; that is, 'What stands as "evidence-rich" practice?'.

Knowing evidence

To understand the idea and relevance of evidence-rich practice for education development, we begin with its meaning. In simple terms:

80 Evidence-informed development

> the word evidence has its origins in a Latin word which means 'to see', the same origin as words such as visible and vision. The e- at the beginning of the word is from the Latin prefix, ex-, meaning 'out of'. So, evidence emerges 'out of what we can see'. Because evidence is something that has been seen, and so verified, it can be used to support a claim, or assertions that something it true.
>
> (Feez and Cox, 2017, p. 2)

In education, evidence is used to make meaning from what is seen; thus, understandings and interpretations made from what is observed are used to improve practices of teaching, learning, professional learning, leading, researching, and evaluating. To gather evidence, means to gather data (or pieces of information) that makes practices and the enabling and constraining conditions *seeable*, or *visible*. But no single source of information is enough, indeed the most robust evidence comes from an accumulation of multiple pieces of information or data that collectively form a sound basis for action and change (Myhill, 2016). While this view might appear to be unwieldly or 'too big', it cautions educators against making decisions based on only one source. Thus, to form a strong or rich evidence-base means having a balance of assessment information (or evidence) upon which one can make a defensible case for changes in their immediate landscape. There is a vast array of materials, documents, artefacts, and measures that can be used as evidence when considering and undertaking educational development, and we will return to these shortly. For us, the key is to find sources of information that *give insights into the issue at hand* as teachers go about learning more about their own practices with the view to improving practices *for* students.

Connecting evidence to the practice landscape: it's about learning

All too often, the discourse of evidence in professional practice and change, and the policies that tout its utility, do not necessarily have sway in the everyday practices of teachers. This is often because the discourse is driven by singular pieces of data or information. This leaves open a pressing need for middle leaders to:

i   understand quality and worthwhile evidence for themselves (in relation of the change initiatives being undertaken in their schools);
ii prioritise evidence as being for learning; and
iii make an impression on teachers about the matter of evidence as they lead the change initiative – in particular its bearing on *actual* development for teachers and students alike and in relation to *actual* student, classroom, and school circumstances and needs.

Raising the matter of evidence with teachers in their professional learning must be framed around and focused on learning – *both* teacher learning *and* student learning. This is a *both-and* proposition. We see the role of the middle leader here as a critical pivot point – it is a role that forges a path towards bridging and brokering the change initiative with and for teachers in schools, so teachers understand the matter of evidence in relation to themselves and their practices. This is a shift that recognises evidence (its form and function) as site-based and supportive of developing best-for-them practices as it relates to the learning of individual teachers and individual students.

This next section then provides an overview of some examples of gathering and analysing evidence.

What counts as evidence? What to collect and how to collect it

Evidence in school-based educational development is recognisably worthwhile when it:

1   directly attends to the focus of the development;
2   is understood in relation to site-based needs and circumstances of individuals and the collective enterprise of the school; and
3   is manageable and reasonable within the normal routines of professional learning, teaching, and learning.

Each of these qualities are necessary but not sufficient on their own for effectual and sustainable change. Particularly, if the evidence does not meet the first two qualities, then it is largely not of use to teachers as a mechanism for responding to their students' needs and circumstances, and if it does not meet the third, then it will be onerous and unsustainable. Thus, all three qualities are essential; if one is overlooked then the programme of professional learning and curriculum development will be ineffective and undoable.

As the next *story from practice* shows, evidence is worthwhile when it is planned for and relates to the professional learning purposes.

Stories from practice: asking rich questions

As part of the *improved questioning* focus of the senior primary teaching team at St Teresa's Primary School, the teachers wanted to ask more 'higher order questions' to promote deep learning and critical thinking among their students in class discussion. To initiate this development focus, in the first cycle of their action research inquiry teachers wanted to understand the nature of the kinds of questions that they actually asked in classes. As Bronwyn (the middle leader responsible for facilitating the activities of the group) said, 'we need to find out what we are currently doing in order to improve and develop'. Brenda (Year 6 teacher), who had a background in interaction analysis through her master's study, suggested that they all audio or video record a lesson, transcribe it, then undertake a thorough analysis using transcript analysis protocols. However, Bronwyn thought that they needed something simpler to begin with. Agreeing, teachers negotiated to conduct a focused lesson observation during an interclass visit in Mark's classroom (one of the team members), while observing his 'teacher-led' whole class discussion. They assigned their next team 'co-plan' session to do the observations. As part of the data collection, the team agreed to record, on a simple tally chart, the kinds of questions the teacher asked.

To get going, Bronwyn cautioned, 'first things first'. So, the substance of questions, and whether these were low, middle, or higher order question, were established during a conversation in the scheduled professional planning meeting prior to the observation. This meeting became an important initial step for the team, as Bronwyn indicated:

> we had to find to common ground. We actually realised that we each had slightly different interpretations of what the types of questions were, how they were phrased, and even how to identify them in a discussion. Michael spoke about 'literal, inferential and critical questions', Joseph mentioned 'right there, between the lines, or going beyond questions'. These discussions made us realise that we knew we could not just go in all guns blazing to do the tally, the observation, without being clear about what it was we meant, we were looking for.

For the team, establishing what each teacher first understood by different types of questions was a necessary step in coming to mutual understandings and consensus about asking rich questions in classroom discussion. The pre-observation discussions, and the reading that informed it, provided stimulus for leading the group to conduct focused observations that, in the end, would be helpful for their professional learning. Bronwyn insisted that what happened after the observations was critical; as she said:

> just conducting classroom observations is not enough, it only matters if there is an actual effect on teacher and student learning and practice. So, it must be followed by a teacher debrief and a 'feedback to feed forward session'. This feedback is a non-negotiable component; it must be focused on what we all have learnt, can learn for ourselves, from the experience and that includes the kids. I stress all because that is the whole point, we all learn something.

As teachers in the team progressed with their understandings about questioning, they came to realise that in practice, questioning in classroom discussions is 'rapid fire'. In later cycles, this awareness led to their eventual undertaking of more in-depth analysis with recordings and transcribing, as suggested by Brenda earlier (noting this approach to transcript analysis is outlined in the second half of this chapter). Bronwyn explained the decision in these terms:

> the tally was really helpful but only as a starting point; it gave us good direction and necessary focus, and a simple overview of the numbers of types of questions we asked. But as we learnt more, we realised that that

information alone was at the surface. What it didn't give us was how the questions influenced the types of responses, answers the kids came up with, or who was asked; like did we ask the same kids the same kinds of questions, that kind of thing. We knew we needed more time, more information, a different approach to take us further at that point.

In a later conversation with Bronwyn, she also cautioned the danger of 'just collecting information for the sake it, teacher's time is pressed enough so we have to make it count'. And as Michael said, 'it is useless if we have so much data we don't know where to start, without having time to look closely at what it means, what it is telling us about the students and their learning, and our teaching too'.

This *story from practice* reflects the three qualities for gathering worthwhile evidence in school-based educational development listed above. It illustrates the need for data to be manageable, focused on learning, and directly related to the professional learning agenda of the teaching team. It also shows how the need for different types of evidence to be collected at different points of the project as learning evolves.

Gathering evidence

Action research is collaborative and evidence-based, thus providing the means for developing a community of practice amongst the teachers in the team, department or group, and ensuring that development is robust and responsive to the needs of the school community (but fundamentally the students). In Figure 5.1, we provide some practical ideas for gathering evidence that support middle leaders develop action research in their schools and provide a stimulus for professional learning dialogues with individuals and groups of teachers.

Examples of evidence which can be collected in educational settings (adapted from Edwards-Groves, Anstey and Bull, 2014; Feez and Cox, 2017)

- formal or informal observations (structured, unstructured and semi-structured), recorded as anecdotal field notes in a diary or journal, in a graphic organiser, a tally or a checklist, classroom walkthroughs, or collegial observations conducted by peers;
- teacher observations (and recorded notes) of a target child or group of students in relation to the focus of development;
- photographs (that can be used for stimulated recall conversations); these may include students taking photographs of 'what helps with their learning, what gets in the way of their learning, what they are interested in, dislike etc, what they find hard or easy at home or at school';
- audio or video recordings of lessons (whole class, small group, student paired conversations);

- transcripts of recorded lessons (teacher-made or professionally transcribed)
- artefacts e.g. student work samples, student drawings of learning experiences in lessons (followed by a conversation – 'tell me about your drawing…'), models;
- documents like policies, curriculum, teachers' programmes;
- surveys, questionnaires, interviews, conferences, focus groups, interest inventories
- 'maps', charts or line drawings, e.g. classroom or playground layout, student movement, sociogram of student interactions;
- teacher reflective writing journal/diary – what is your project about? What question are you asking of yourself? Why do you want to change this? What has surprised you in the change process? What has puzzled you? What questions to you still have? What do the parents say?
- numerical measurements, e.g. of time taken, distance or area covered, tasks completed, attendance, classroom quiz, term assignments, end of year examinations, or national test scores (e.g. NAPLAN), scales (e.g. of attitudes, student interests).

Transcripts as evidence: recording, transcribing and analysing lessons

One of the issues facing middle leaders is how to support teachers to analyse evidence, in particular how to analyse (and so to learn from) audio or video recorded lessons which are a becoming a more commonly used strategy in understanding and critiquing professional practice. This next section provides a more detailed example that aims to supplement the sketchier ideas presented earlier; here we aim to provide a deep and robust practical way that transcripts as evidence can be used and understood.

Transcripts as instructive professional learning tools

To stimulate a focus on practice in teacher development, middle leaders often utilise techniques such as peer observations, classroom walkthroughs, taking photos as visual snapshots of 'critical' moments in lessons, or video recording lessons to ground their 'coaching'. Each of these techniques are useful tools that provoke deeper level thought beyond a simple recall activity. Less common is the use of transcripts, in particular making and examining one's own transcripts. This section focuses on the educative power of transcripts (Edwards-Groves, 2003), although their use requires more time. As a starting point for professional learning, making a preliminary transcript is a pre-project source of evidence that assists teachers to find a focus for development for themselves (Edwards-Groves and Davidson, 2017) that acts as baseline evidence of practice that also acts as a lever for change.

What you need to know about practice. Why transcripts?

As one of the 'actors' in lessons – that is, one of the participants – teachers cannot realistically stand back and, at the same time, be an effective interpreter or analyst of her/his own practice during a lesson. A second phase is needed; one that grounds and directs teacher reflection and enables them to revisit (view, hear, or reflect on) their lesson in a focused and generative way. Often classroom walkthroughs and focused observations by middle leaders or trusted peers can assist teachers in this process, but this relies on the adeptness of others to also interpret teaching practices in the rapid fire *happeningness* and immediacy of a lesson. Recorded lessons and transcripts, particularly teacher-made transcripts of their own lessons (Edwards-Groves and Davidson, 2017), help teachers build capacity in that they establish for themselves the issues for development. Transcripts make visible what actually happens since lessons *unfold in sequential turns of talk*. Fundamentally, teachers need to know what happens in their lessons in order to develop and change.

Transcripts form important pieces of evidence that provide a turn-by-turn record of the teaching and learning practices that shape how lessons happen (what actually takes place, what discipline language is used by teachers and students, how teachers and students respond and relate to one another). Specifically, transcripts show how the talk between teachers and students in lessons forms a fundamental connection to the curriculum (or discipline goals); and at the same time, it creates the core of the interpersonal, social and intellectual relationships between teachers and students. By making and reading transcripts of their own lessons, it has been found that teachers learn that the ways that their classroom talk is a main tool for teaching, for thinking, and for learning (Edwards-Groves, 2003; Edwards-Groves and Davidson, 2017). So regardless of what texts or curriculum documents are used for example, it is through the talk and patterns of teacher-student interaction in lessons that the teaching and learning is enacted and made obvious to all (or some) in the lesson.

Teacher-made transcripts provides teachers with additional opportunities to systematically and more critically revisit, reflect on, and evaluate their lessons (Edwards-Groves and Davidson, 2017). This is because the actual process of transcribing the recordings requires teachers to consider their teaching a number of times through the process:

i   First, they experience it in doing the lesson itself.
ii Second, as they listen to or view the audio or video recorded version, they encounter it again.
iii Third, in transcribing it they listen to every word in sequence that they then write or type. This provides another opportunity to carefully listen and closely observe: (i) what they say and do, and how they relate to the students; and (ii) what students say and do, and how they relate to the teacher and to one another.

86 *Evidence-informed development*

These multiple 'passes' through the lesson experience reveals to them the actual content and pedagogical processes and patterns used in their own lessons (rather than hearing about best practice suggestions from external programmes). How transcripts benefit an individual's professional learning is captured here in this teacher's comment:

> As a result of reading my own lesson transcripts ... I now know that a lesson really relies on more than the syllabus, or the books or the activities I planned or like to do. It is more about how I interact with my students—how I engage students in their learning through my talk. I didn't realise the importance of it until I looked at some of those transcripts. I now continually listen to myself and ask 'What did the kids hear?' and 'Is that what I want them to focus on?'
>
> (Senior Primary Teacher)

Reading and *rereading* transcripts enable teachers to 'work over' lessons (the transcript or video recorded lesson) for what is revealed on a moment-by-moment, turn-by-turn basis. Although they can take a lot of time and energy, we know that transcripts can form an important piece of evidence about teaching practices, and for professional development (Edwards-Groves, 2003). They are a helpful tool for teachers in their professional learning, by not only helping them understand and interpret their own classroom practices by revealing their *everyday* teaching and learning routines and instructional focuses, but assist teachers to establish *for themselves* what is effective and ultimately, what is achieved intellectually, interactionally, and culturally by their lessons (Edwards-Groves and Davidson, 2017). They are a stimulus for professional learning conversations that allow teachers to reflect, in a focused way, about whether similar or different approaches might be useful for student learning in future lessons.

Thus, we believe transcripts provide evidence for teachers to become self-aware, and support them to understand and so interact with others (Northouse, 2013). Importantly, for teacher professional learning, transcripts provide a springboard for committed action, continued growth, on-going learning and focused inquiry because their own practice is the foundation from which they are building the change initiative (Edwards-Groves, 2003; Edwards-Groves and Davidson, 2017).

Recording, transcribing and analysing transcripts

Since complete lessons transcripts are long and extensive, it is neither profitable nor indeed possible to generate a large quantity of transcript data. So to begin, we recommend that teachers select one lesson to record for a complete transcription; later teachers may focus on transcribing one phase or segment of a lesson (e.g. lesson introductions, whole class discussion, or a small group discussion, or the lesson conclusion – the summary or review phase). Because of this, the process could proceed along the following lines:

Evidence-informed development 87

Steps for recording, transcribing and analysing: a 'how to' guide for teachers

1 *Equipment:* teachers don't need specialised recording equipment to make a recording as long as the sound quality is good (although if it is available then it can be used of course); as shown in Figure 5.1, everyday recording devices like phones, iPads or MP4 players, a home camcorder or *Go Pros* can be used; make sure that teachers check battery life.
2 *Personnel:* consider who might do the recording – this might be the middle leader, a critical friend, member of a teaching team, or a device might simply be set up on a stand or tripod (as shown in Figure 5.2 below).
3 *Recording:* test equipment thoroughly before recording complete lessons, students group conversations, or whole class discussions (note: be aware of outside activities like building or maintenance; consider the position of microphones for example not too close to computers, open windows). After setting up the equipment and before recording, establish and write down the lesson focus.
4 *Transcribing:* first, make a full 'word-only' verbatim transcript (that is a word-by-word, turn-by-turn record of who says what when). Make a note of which student is talking. This is a systematic process, but a bit time consuming (teachers might complain, but in the end be glad they did it). For selected segments (like the whole class discussion, or the lesson plenary) use the transcript conventions (in Appendix 4) which note the more

Figure 5.1 Simple recording equipment

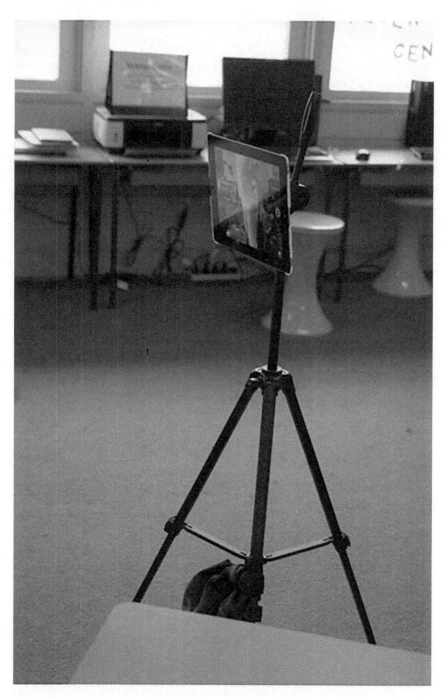

Figure 5.2 Camera (iPad) stand set-up

precise turns, literal statements, pronunciation, as well as take account of such interaction features as pauses, volume, interruptions and overlapping talk and so on. Making a set of transcripts from recorded lessons (e.g. of consecutive lessons in a unit of work) helps teachers establish their own patterns or routines.
5   *Scanning for patterns*: then guide the teachers to scan the entire transcript to obtain a sense of the main features of their talk. Listen to or observe the lessons for a sense of the 'whole'. It is recommended to listen to the entire recording a number of times and *read* each transcription a number of times to provide a context for the emergence of specific patterns, problem spots, individual student contributions, etc.
6   *Analysing*: this phase aims to have teachers understand what they, the teacher, and their students are *actually* saying, rather than what is expected to be said. The teacher studies the transcripts to determine *themes*. This involves a thorough scrutiny of the sequences of turns so teachers themselves can elicit the essence of their talk, meanings, consistencies and inconsistencies, places where there is trouble and so on. Make notes entailing a list of issues related to the topic and the structure of lessons; making brief notes and highlighting particular segments on the transcripts is useful. These highlighted sections are the beginnings of 'codes' that form common or central threads for further thought, investigation, and action.
7   *Collaborative analysis involves middle leaders beginning by asking teachers*:

- *What do you notice?*
- *Who is talking?*
- *What is happening here?*
- *What is happening in each turn?*
- *Who is talking? When?*
- *What 'talk moves' are used by you? Students? How often?*
- *What evidence is there that students have opportunities to:*
    - *Sustain the point?*
    - *Talk to each other?*
    - *Extend and respond to the thinking of others?*
    - *Provide reasons, justifications?*
    - *Challenge the thinking of others?*
    - *Question others?*
    - *Revoice and repeat?*
    - *Reflect on and evaluate learning? How? When?*

8   *Remember when reading transcripts, it is important to try to:

- Suspend judgements on whether or not you think it is a good/bad lesson, or what the intention might be. Look at the lesson in terms of *what the students seem to take to be going on, what the students show*, rather than what your own or the teacher's intention might be; think of

student contributions as indications of what they understand to be going on.
- Treat classroom lessons as jointly produced by the teacher *and* the students (as they have a part in it too).
- Think of a lesson as an interaction that is built up in sequences of turns; from its onset consider how it begins, progresses, and ends, and what possible *lessons* are learnt, what topics are spoken about (language used or sayings), what activities are being done (or doings) and how people are relating to one another across the sequence (or relatings).
- Find what is shown or made *relevant or obvious* in the talk – what is actually going on; do students hear what the lesson is about; how speakers speak and how they hear one another; is someone dominant over another.

9 *Negotiating a programme for professional development and change:* each teacher's tentative themes help to identify recommendations and pathways for development and change. A summary might be written up to incorporate the main themes drawn from the transcript evidence – this 'pins down' the focus for development and change for the teacher. Teachers may work with supportive colleagues or the middle leader in negotiating and planning specific arenas for changing their own practice. The true value of collegial or middle leader support cannot be overstated (regular contact is recommended). Therefore, be particularly sensitive to teachers working in isolation. *To move teachers forward in their thinking and action, middle leaders can ask:*

- *What do you need to do differently? Why?*
- *What can you show? Describe? Tell others about your lessons through a focus on talk in the transcripts?* (Note other questions appear in Appendix 5.)

10 *Acting on evidence*: For evidence-informed change, an individually negotiated plan can be drawn up to ensure a focused programme of professional development is undertaken. The plan can be as simple or as detailed as teachers feel necessary. Some teachers may opt to record and transcribe further lessons for the purposes of evaluation, review and reflection over time. This part of the process in the professional learning project enables teachers (and you) to compare and contrast lesson practices, to establish firm evidence of development and practice change.

Videos and transcripts of lessons are important pieces of evidence for teachers in their professional learning. It has been shown that analysing their own teaching practices through lesson videos and transcripts, teachers are not only able to identify the categories for change, but are able to recognise the need for change, change, and show it in their practice (Edwards-Groves, 2003). Teachers also can recognise and account for changes in practice in relation to the way they managed and organised the topics for talk, and the structural features of lessons. Teachers might need to be reminded to take particular care with sharing videos or images of children beyond the professional learning activity; this may be a breach of ethical practice so it is also important to delete films stored on phones or iPad after transcribing them, and to keep them safe maybe on a password protected location.

In summary, teachers can, by exposure to their own transcripts, orient to changing their conceptualisation of what counts as a lesson, what counts in their lessons and how they show it in their talk. Importantly, teachers begin to consider that 'a lesson' is an interactive practice, acknowledging that it is through the classroom talk and discussions that the work of lessons gets done. Furthermore, they begin to consider the importance of talk for making the curriculum available to the diverse group of learners within their own (and varied) contexts.

Conclusion

In this chapter we have tried to highlight the importance of evidence to inform and ground professional learning and curriculum development in schools, and the key role that the middle leader has in facilitating and driving evidenced-informed development. Worthwhile evidence needs to be focused on the issue at hand, responsive to and insightful of local needs and conditions, but also manageable within the busy routines of school life. As middle leaders, the challenge is to support your teaching team as they engage in a school's site based professional learning and curriculum development in response to the insights of meaningful evidence. This means avoiding the dangerous trap of looking for some form of 'best practice' that can be imported from outside.

Theory-into-practice (TIPs): questions for reflection and discussion

1 Discuss how government and systemic agendas around 'data' and 'evidence' impacted your role and work as a middle leader?
2 In your context, how has the collection of 'data' impacted teaching practices? How could a focus on 'evidence' be helpful?
3 How can you re-imagine your middle leading practices to make more useful and manageable use of evidence?
4 Reread the *stories from practice* in this chapter. Draw out the key learning points described; discuss their value for supporting teachers to align practice development with student learning. Develop and trial one of the approaches mentioned.

References

Biesta, G. (2010). 'Why 'What Works' Still Won't Work: From Evidence-Based Education to Value-Based Education', *Studies in Philosophy and Education*, 29(5), 491–503.

Dewey, J. (1938). *Experience and Education*. Michigan, US: Kappa Dets Pi.

Edwards-Groves, C. (2003). *On task: Focused literacy learning*. Newtown, Sydney, NSW: Primary English Teaching Association Australia (PETAA).

Edwards-Groves, C. (2013). 'Creating spaces for critical transformative dialogues: Legitimising discussion groups as professional practice', *Australian Journal of Teacher Education*, 38(12), 17–34.

Edwards-Groves, C. and Davidson, C. (2017). *Becoming a Meaning Maker: Talk and Interaction in the Dialogic Classroom*. Newtown, Sydney, NSW: Primary English Teaching Association Australia (PETAA).

Edwards-Groves, C., Anstey, M. and Bull, G. (2014). *Classroom Talk: Understanding dialogue, pedagogy and practice*. Newtown, Sydney, NSW: Primary English Teaching Association Australia (PETAA).

Feez, S. and Cox, R. (2017). 'Understanding research and evidence: a guide for teachers', PETAA Paper 209. Newtown, Sydney, NSW: Primary English Teaching Association Australia (PETAA).

Hammersley, M. (2009). 'Against the ethicists: on the evils of ethical regulation', *International Journal of Social Research Methodology*, 12(3), 211–225.

Kemmis, S., McTaggart, R. and Nixon, R. (2014). *The action research planner. Doing critical participatory action research*. Singapore: Springer Education.

Kemmis, S., Wilkinson, J., Edwards-Groves, C., Hardy, I., Grootenboer, P. and Bristol, L. (2014). *Changing Practices, Changing Education*. Singapore: Springer Education.

Morris, E. (2011). 'Labour could build trust by committing to evidence in education policies', *The Guardian*. www.theguardian.com/education/2011/sep/26/estelle-evidence-interpret-ofsted-pisa-timms.

Myhill, D. (2016). Grammar for writing. In H. de Silva Joyce and S. Feez, *Exploring Literacies: Theory, Research and Practice* (pp. 320–322). London: Palgrave Macmillan.

Northouse, P. (2013). *Introduction. In Leadership: Theory and practice*, 6th edition. Thousand Oaks: SAGE.

Further reading

Edwards-Groves, C. (2014). 'Talk Moves: A repertoire of practices for productive classroom dialogue'. Invited article in PETAA PAPERs 195. Newtown, Sydney, NSW: Primary English Teaching Association Australia (PETAA).

Moss, C. and Brookhart, S. (2015). *Formative Classroom Walkthroughs: How principals and teachers collaborate to raise student achievement*. Virginia, US: ASCD.

6 Middle leading in practice

In the first five chapters of this book we have outlined a range of ideas, concepts and principles related to middle leadership in educational contexts. Now, in this penultimate chapter we want to discuss these things in a more integrated and practical manner. To this end, first, two case studies are introduced – one set in a primary school and the other in a secondary context, and these will be developed and used as a unifying thread throughout the chapter. The main aim here is to help the middle leader practise their middle leading – and to do it in the light of all that has gone before. Case studies are presented to show how others have moved forward. Specifically, the discussion will focus on practising middle leading with a community of colleagues and by engaging in evidence-based local development.

Middle leading in practice: cases for study

Before we move into the middle leading practices that shaped the two cases for study, first we introduce the background context and details for each case. These cases for study are more substantial examples than those presented as 'stories from practice' in previous chapters. After each case is previewed, we will then revisit and elaborate on each case through the key ideas as the chapter progresses.

Riverbank Primary School case study: whole school project bringing teacher dialogue and student dialogue into mathematics instruction

Suzanne was an experienced Year 2 teacher and the instructional leader for literacy and numeracy development in her large regional city primary school located in a highly disadvantaged suburb. As well as teaching her Year 2 students, part of her role involved supporting the professional development of the 33 teachers in the school. In a school executive leader's planning meeting that included Suzanne, the team decided that to improve student learning in mathematics, teachers needed to focus on having the students be able to communicate their thinking more effectively in class discussions.

94 Middle leading in practice

Suzanne had previously been involved in a year-long regional action research project focused on using dialogic pedagogies for instructional efficacy in literacy; this project was facilitated by researchers from the local university. Suzanne had decided that to improve student's mathematics content knowledge, she would begin by applying what she had learnt about facilitating student learning by changing monologic teacher questioning in whole class activities to questions that focused on providing more opportunities for students to provide extended responses. This, she argued, would promote student's deeper engagement in learning through an enhanced capacity to communicate mathematical ideas and concepts. She modelled the facilitation approaches she had learnt from working with the university researchers to her work with the teaching teams.

Mathematics in high school case study: Gavin (HoD Mathematics) leading pedagogical change

Gavin was the Head of the Mathematics department in a medium-sized secondary school in a relatively low socio-economic community. The mathematics department included eight teachers, and together they taught 34 classes of Year 8 to 12 students (aged 13 to 19 years). The school's mathematics results in formal assessments had been adequate without ever being outstanding, but many students dropped the subject, or took it at a 'lower level', as soon as they could. In short, the students did okay, but in general they disliked mathematics, thought it was largely irrelevant, and many disengaged as soon as they could. The school principal was a former mathematics teacher, and while he was keen for an improvement in mathematics engagement and performance, he did not want any 'radical changes' that would impact senior school exam results.

The teachers in the department had a range of teaching styles and approaches from traditional teacher-directed to more cooperative and based on investigations, and they ranged in experience from Alison – a first year teacher through to Mirkka with over 30 years in the classroom. In the past they had used department meetings to cover administrative matters (e.g. systems for resource use) and to manage required developments (e.g. implementing a new national curriculum).

Developing a community

Throughout the chapters of this book we have already discussed the importance and centrality of developing and sustaining collegiality for professional and curriculum development. This has been highlighted and promoted through a range of conceptual terms including 'professional learning communities (PLCs)' (DuFour and Eaker, 1998), 'communities of practice' (Lave and Wenger, 1991), and 'communicative spaces' (Habermas, 1996). Whatever the title or term used to refer to the group of professionals (i.e. teachers) working together, it is clear that it is more than just a meeting or an administrative grouping.

For a middle leader, it is clear that their work by its very nature involves working with colleagues, but this also provides one of the greatest leadership challenges. Specifically, middle leaders are often promoted to their leadership positions because they had been recognised as a good classroom teacher. But as a classroom teacher they had 'control' over the educational practices that occurred, but now as a middle leader they are responsible for the teaching and learning across a range of classrooms – most of which are taught by other people, and so are outside the middle leader's direct influence! Put simply, a middle leader cannot realise good teaching and learning in their department or syndicate alone, so building collegiality and a community of professionals is not optional! It has to be a shared project to engage in curriculum development and professional learning.

In the previous chapters we discussed and illustrated a range of features that middle leaders need to foster and sustain to build collegiality (e.g. trust, communication), so here we want to exemplify and discuss these through the two case studies.

Case for study: developing and using PLCs at Riverbank Primary School

To work with the whole staff on the dialogic pedagogies in mathematics project, it was necessary for Suzanne to consider how she would bring all the grade teaching teams together 'to be on the same page, but to honour their individuality at the same time'. To begin, Suzanne had to decide whether working in the established grade teams or newly-formed across-grade teams would be the most effective. Both had merits, both had problems. After consulting the executive team, they decided that to be truly collaborative it might be best to discuss the options with the whole staff. After negotiation with the staff, a preference for working in grade-based teaching teams was established. As a group, this tack would be a more efficient way to facilitate both the desired change and the development of the PLC needed for the kind of intensive work that the project required. As Suzanne said, 'in the end, you can't just throw people together and expect cohesion; trust is needed, and this is built over time as people work with one another'.

After an introductory whole day, whole school input session on the nature of dialogic instruction in mathematics that was facilitated by Suzanne, teaching teams met again for a two-hour after school meeting to plan the details and timeline of data gathering and analysis activities for their projects. At these meetings, teachers came to consensus about the kind of evidence that was required to demonstrate student and teacher development, to prepare their 'theories-of-action-in practice' and to make a schedule for future meetings and activities. These initial planning meetings laid the grounds for building a collegial climate needed for collaborative respectful decision making.

Case for study: developing a shared focus in the department

As was noted in the introduction to Gavin's case study, in the mathematics department there were a diverse range of teaching approaches and styles, and years of experience. For Gavin, it was important that they could develop a shared focus for their curriculum and professional development, but also still allow for their own teaching philosophies and approaches, and not 'squeeze everyone to be the same – that would be deprofessionalising!'. He did not believe that there was one single way to best teach mathematics, and that it was actually a strength of the department that they had different styles.

So, as he started his second year as the HoD, Gavin organised for a *department day*, where the teaching team met to plan for the year. The teachers in the department were already warm and friendly towards one another as colleagues, but they had not really worked professionally in a collaborative manner. To facilitate the dialogue and collaboration on the day, Gavin had organised to go off-site so they were not interrupted, and organised for refreshments and catering to be provided.

As a group, they quickly agreed that there was an issue with student disengagement with mathematics, and that this was the biggest concern that they had to deal with as a department. However, from this readily accepted position, the challenge was to find a shared understanding about how to address it, and then where exactly to start. To prompt discussion, Gavin shared a short article (five pages long) about student engagement which they all read, and then after five minutes of individual personal reflection, the teachers engaged in an open discussion. After about 45 minutes they came to an unforced and shared consensus that a key issue was 'relevance' and being able to show that the mathematics the students were learning was useful. This became their initial focus for the development of their pedagogy and curriculum.

After a break, teachers reconvened and 'brainstormed' as many ideas as they could garner, and then they worked to narrow down to what they would do in the first unit of work (as their first action research cycle). It was decided that each teacher would include a relatively simple applied mathematical activity that involved an authentic application of the mathematical concept being taught in the first unit, with one of their junior classes. At this stage the teachers then split into those that would focus on Year 8 and those that would focus on Year 9, and they developed the first task together. Finally, they came back together and actually did the mathematical tasks themselves, and then decided that in the first cycle, they would each collect a range of 10 student work samples from the applied task from their class as evidence to inform their reflective evaluation of the initiative, and to do a personal review of their students' samples so they could have an evidence-based dialogue at their staff meeting in Week 3.

Key practices in developing a community

As was noted previously, as a middle leader you are reliant on your teaching colleagues to provide quality education across the classes for which you have oversight. Although as a middle leader you might well be a fantastic teacher, a lone great teacher cannot achieve the educational goals of a school, department, or syndicate – it needs a community of professional colleagues.[1] Of course, establishing the necessity of a teaching team is relatively easy – actually developing and sustaining it is a much more challenging proposition for the middle leader!

As we have noted throughout the book, the leading practices that are required to develop and sustain a professional community will be shaped and responsive to local needs and conditions – there is not a best practice model to follow or a set of 'foolproof' steps. That said, here we want to outline some ideas that might be helpful, together with some examples and tools, so middle leaders can develop their own leading practices in their particular school site. The four inter-related key features we will focus on are: (1) developing a sense of 'we'; (2) having a shared focus; (3) using time; and (4) trust.

Developing a sense of 'we'

A middle leader, often in contrast to a principal or positional head, still has a substantial teaching role, and so while they are undertaking their leading, they are also teaching – as we have noted previously, they are like a playing captain in a sports team rather than a manager or team coach. This means that there is a sense of 'we' because everyone is engaged in the core educational business of teaching and learning. However, in schools we often refer to classes as if they 'belong' to a teacher; e.g. 'Ms Downs takes 11C for English'. This is often exacerbated by school structures where teachers have their classrooms, and exercise their professional autonomy behind the closed classroom door with their classes (Hargreaves, 1994). Indeed, teacher professionalism is important, but we argue that professionalism is shared quality, and is enhanced when teachers work together.

One simple but profound shift is to change the language from 'my class' and 'my students' to 'our classes' and 'our students'. In practice, this shared sense of responsibility for the learning and teaching in all classes across the school, department, syndicate, or group means that any development or issues are considered and resolved collectively, engaging the multi-faceted resources of the staff in the team. So, if a new curriculum is introduced at a particular Year level, then staff beyond the immediate teachers involved would be involved in the course development, or if there were some classroom management issues with a particular class, then all the teachers in the group would share responsibility to support the specific teacher and students concerned.

Another way that teaching teams can develop a sense of community is by engaging in shared discipline-based activities. In the example of Gavin and the mathematics department above, after they designed the mathematics tasks, they actually did the mathematics activities themselves. At the time, one of the teachers commented that, 'it had been ages since I'd actually done any maths myself', and once they got past their initial self-consciousness, they all quite enjoyed it. Gavin then included a mathematics problem (selected and prepared by each teacher on a rostered basis) that the staff worked on at every second staff meeting. In other teacher groups there are a range of shared activities that could be undertaken, including subject-based tasks like doing some mathematics or physical education teachers playing a game, to more education-focused pursuits like reading through and discussing a shared book.

Having a shared focus

Related to 'developing a sense of we' is having a shared focus. This can be at a broad level, but also in terms of annual planning. While it might seem obvious, in broad terms the focus should be on student learning. It would be difficult to find an educator that would disagree with this single-minded concentration, but in how middle leader's work unfolds in practice, it can get lost. So, what is important here is that the focus on student learning is evident in the unfolding structures and practices of the teaching team. Often what this will entail is a deliberate and intentional shift by middle leaders (and senior leaders) away from using prime time and resources for managerial and bureaucratic work, and towards learning and teaching. This can be achieved in a number of ways, including dealing with administrative matters by electronic means, and intentionally shaping department meeting agendas around learning and teaching.

In both examples of middle leaders Suzanne and Gavin, teacher professional development days were held prior to the students returning to school to develop the focus for the upcoming year – in Suzanne's case, this was the focus on promoting dialogic pedagogies in primary mathematics lessons to facilitate students' capacities for communicating mathematical ideas in extended responses; and in Gavin's case, the focus on helping students appreciate the usefulness of mathematics to promote deeper and more long-standing engagement. Developing the shared focus was clearly made under a broad umbrella emphasis on student learning, but much tighter and more particular, in order to shape the specific attention for the year. It is important to note that research has found that when teachers work together with a quite particular focus, their pedagogy tends to develop more broadly, and this is not the case when teachers across a team have scattered foci.

Using time

If anything is going to confound educational development in schools, then it will often be time, or a lack thereof! So, for middle leaders, perhaps the most important resource for their work that demands specific attention is time (Grootenboer, 2018). This relates as much to 'developing a community' as every other aspect of middle leading. Fundamentally, following on from the previous points, it is about using time on the shared key focus of student learning.

Perhaps the most overt way this can be actioned is through the time available through regular staff/department/syndicate meetings. While there is a myriad of administrative and managerial work that can fill hours of community time, if education is truly the focus of the team (as it should be) then the precious time available needs to primarily be spent on learning and teaching matters.

'Time is of the essence', said Suzanne. Bob, the principal at Riverbank, agreed. He realised that to be effective, Suzanne should be allocated additional time in her daily schedule for planning the PL meetings, preparing material resources, sourcing relevant literature, for having individual teacher analysis meetings and for conducting coaching conversations with the teaching teams during their co-plan meetings. Bob also reassigned the weekly staff meeting to a focus on professional development. This additional time meant Suzanne was relieved from her Year 2 class for a day a week to develop the interconnected layers of support that met the varying needs of both the individual teachers, the grade level teams and the project focus on dialogic pedagogies in mathematics.

Suzanne knew that changing teachers' classroom discussion practices is a time consuming, but often taken-for-granted dimension of a teacher's daily work. So, she negotiated with Bob an additional co-plan meeting time per term for each of the teacher teams so that the teachers had the necessary time for deep thinking and collaborative professional dialogues about this complex area of teaching. Bob trusted Suzanne's knowledge and instinct on this matter and allocated the necessary funding for teacher release for the additional time for teachers to meet. This commitment by Bob validated the project by enabling both the teachers and Suzanne to invest more dedicated time to their learning.

Relational trust

We have already discussed trust in some detail, so here we just want to reiterate how crucial it is to middle leaders as they lead effective site-based professional learning. Although it can be elusive, without trust the wheels of collegiality will quickly grind to a halt, and while it can take a long time to develop, and thoughtfulness to sustain, it can be lost in a moment through a careless word or inconsiderate action. Trust is precious, so as a middle leader do all you can to develop and sustain it.

The project at Riverbank Primary School involved teachers visiting each other's classrooms and for video-recording mathematics lessons that became the substance of joint de-brief and analysis meetings. To be productive required a high level of trust between members of the teams and in the professional learning process Suzanne designed (with their help). It also required a high degree of trust in Suzanne's knowledge of: (i) dialogic pedagogies; (ii) mathematics curriculum and the instructional methods for efficacy; and (iii) the processes for facilitating change. As one of the teachers in the school reflected, 'The way teachers' manage their discussions is very personal, we all work differently, but Suzanne has this kind, but genuine way, of valuing and supporting everyone to reflect hard on what they are doing. We trust her way because she also shows she trusts us to take it seriously, the more we met, the easier it was to open up about our own struggles.' Mutual trust as described here was established by and through working with each other.

Engaging in evidence-based development

One of the key aspects of a middle leader's role is to develop and sustain meaningful, practical and effective ways to collect and use evidence to inform on-going curriculum and staff development. Again, we will not reiterate the points made in previous chapters about the importance of curriculum development and professional learning being informed, and responsive to, evidence, but rather we will focus on some practicalities of evidence collection and analysis. The first is to suggest that what is required is not necessarily deep and robust data, as might be required for a PhD study, but rather evidence that directly informs understandings about what is happening in the site. In this sense, it is often more like the evidence that might inform a historical account or a newspaper article, rather than statistical data that might be used for a scientific experiment. This is not to say that the evidence should be flimsy and weak, but rather that it needs to be 'fit for purpose', informative, and manageable as part of a teachers' work.

Case for study: using classroom walkthroughs and lesson recordings as evidence in Riverbank Primary

To begin the project on dialogic pedagogies in mathematics, it was critical for teachers to establish how they currently conduct their whole class discussions; that is to collect some baseline information from which to gauge development. To initiate the process, Suzanne set up classroom observations through the 'classroom walkthrough' – teachers negotiated who, when, and what the focus would be. Classroom walkthroughs were generally brief (up to about 20 minutes during the discussion phase of the lesson); observations were focused on the teacher's questioning moves, and the subsequent students' mathematical responses in the discussions. Sometimes Suzanne was involved, but sometimes she covered the classes for other teachers so they could participate in the classroom walkthrough visits. After these sessions, teachers (individually or collectively) used the information yielded in the classroom observation (often recorded in checklists or teacher-made notes) as the substance of their professional learning dialogues. Through their professional discussions, Suzanne found that the teacher's comments were becoming increasingly in-depth and focused on improvement as they delved deeper into how to promote genuine student mathematical learning through more developed classroom discussions.

After their initial rounds of observations (conducted over a term), teachers in the teams decided to go deeper into ideas about what constitutes a dialogic discussion. From previous experience, Suzanne knew that video-recording one's lessons generated evidence about practice that subsequently created a springboard for professional change. Although confronting for some teachers at the beginning, the recordings of lessons generated firm grounds for teachers to 'step back' to reflect on what they were doing, what the students were doing and what changes were needed to ensure that the questioning in their mathematics lessons were more dialogic. Teachers, in their smaller teaching teams, took turns to share their videos and lead a discussion about what changes they were trialling in their lessons; the others in the group posed questions about their observations of the lessons. Suzanne's role in these discussions was critical, as she led by example to keep the focus on each teacher's pedagogical change and development.

Case for study: how do we know if it has made a difference in their mathematical learning?

For Gavin and the team in the mathematics department, they had made some initial plans about how they would begin, but of course they wanted to know if the new activities actually made a difference. At first, they came up with a wide range of ideas, but it soon became clear that this would not be manageable within the existing school and class routines and structures, so they agreed, for the initial round, to 'keep it simple' – hence the decision noted above to collect a range of 10 student work samples from the first shared activity. This was seen as useful and practicable evidence because it: (1) reflected explicitly the students' learning; (2) was already created in the class; (3) focused on the issue at hand; and (4) teachers could analyse and reflect on their own evidence prior to the meeting where they collectively considered the outcomes of the first cycle. Also, related to the point above about building trust, this first round meant the teachers were still able to collect and consider their class-based evidence privately, and this fairly 'soft' opening to the action research processes allowed staff to warm towards the practices and build confidence and a foundation of trust before perhaps delving collaboratively a little deeper.

After the first cycle the department met to share their individual findings and insights, and they found that the work samples indicated a general level of engagement (e.g. students were quite fulsome in their responses to the activities) and the included mathematical concepts seemed to be understood, although perhaps only within the context of the particular activities. Also, while the teachers did not explicitly collect any evidence related to the students' enjoyment and participation in the lesson, they all seemed to think that the students were positive at the time. With this in mind, for the second round the group decided to follow a similar process to the first cycle, but this time to also collect 10 work samples from a related follow-up more formal mathematics task, that the students would do the next day, to see if there was any learning transfer from the 'applied task' to the more formal mathematics task. Initially Gavin was a little disappointed with this decision made by the group, as it seemed to move a little away from the central issue of disengagement, but he did not override the groups democratic decision-making process, because he felt that the 'development of trust and confidence with and in one another' was more important. Again, the student work samples were reflectively considered and analysed by each teacher, and the findings and insights shared at the following department meeting. However, Gavin also felt that the levels of trust and confidence were growing and so he gently suggested that in the third cycle they might include some classroom observations, and he began the negotiations with the Deputy Principal so this would be possible (in terms of releasing staff when and where necessary).

In the third cycle, where once again they developed and employed another problem-solving applied mathematical task, but this time one staff member observed and collected data related to student engagement as one of their teaching colleagues used the activity. The data collected was very specific and defined by a recording sheet. Simply, every three minutes the visiting teacher would note the phase and action at that time (e.g. introduction – teacher explaining), and then scan the room to make a quick count of how many students seemed to be 'engaged' or 'actively participating' (e.g. 17 of 25). Then, at a convenient time after the lesson the two teachers met, and the one observing teacher simply gave the other the data as recorded on the sheet. The teacher who presented the lesson could then initiate a discussion with the observing, asking for clarification of what might have been happening at the time. The observing teacher did not offer any evaluation of the teacher's practice in the lesson or comment about any other aspect of the lesson. This was then used by the teacher, along with the selected work samples from the lesson, to reflectively consider the activity, and specifically how it impacted engagement and mathematical learning. Of note, Gavin was the first to have a colleague in his classroom to observe, and he asked the most junior member of the teaching team to be his observer.

Using evidence effectively

The nature and forms of evidence employed in school-based action research is vast and varied, but as should be clear – it needs to be informative, credible and manageable. For many, as they embark on this evidence-based approach to professional and curriculum development, the effective collection and use of evidence and data can be a little overwhelming. Perhaps the key thing to remember here then is, KEEP IT SIMPLE! In our experience, there tends to be a problem with middle leaders and schools making this aspect overly complicated, too cumbersome, and unwieldy. If indeed, you are using an external critical friend, then often one of the ways they can be most useful is in providing ideas and support around evidence collection and analysis.

Collecting and generating evidence

Considering these things, evidence can be found or generated in three broad ways:

1   materials and documents that are already produced as a normal part of a lesson or educational work (e.g. student work samples, test scores, department meeting minutes);

2   recording aspects of activities that are a normal part of a lesson or educational work (e.g. observations of lesson, photos of students working on a task); and
3   specific evidence collection activities (e.g. a simple student survey).

These all have their place, but as much as possible it is worth relying primarily on evidence collection from the normal routines and practices – this is evidence to inform development. If the collection of evidence becomes too onerous or time consuming, then it is unlikely to be sustainable in the long term, and perhaps more importantly, the evidence from everyday educational practice is most likely to be the most valid in terms of revealing what is actually happening.

In the case of Gavin and the Secondary School Mathematics Department, for the first two cycles the evidence was gathered from material – student work samples – that had already been produced as part of the lessons concerned; teachers only had to make copies of selected pieces. In the third cycle they included some more intentional evidence collection through classroom observations, but this was only once the teachers involved were ready for the more collaborative, and more challenging, prospective of having a colleague watching you teach. It is also critical to note the simplicity of the data collected – a simple count of how many students appeared to be actively participating. Importantly here, there was careful management of the observations (through an observation sheet) that focused the evidence collection of the specific features concerned, and helped the teachers to appreciate that it was not about judging and evaluating their performance per se.

The importance of this in terms of maintaining trust and a sense of collegiality should not be under estimated. Reciprocity is a key part of trust. To this end Gavin also showed his trust in his teaching peers by being the first to have someone come into his classroom to observe. Finally, it should be noted that after the fourth cycle, the teaching team thought that it was important to ascertain the students' views on these new activities in their mathematics programme, so they prepared a short (one A5 sheet) and simple survey (four Likert scale questions) that the students completed in their mathematics classes. Their responses were aggregated, and these were used to inform the subsequent cycle where they overtly addressed the issues that emerged in their ongoing minor reforms to their pedagogy and curriculum.

Analysing evidence to inform practice

Once the evidence is collected through the cycle, the next consideration is how to analyse and use it to provide insights about what is happening. Of course, this will depend on the evidence or data collected, but in general the key is to try and understand what has occurred vis-à-vis the topic or focus of the inquiry, and in particular in response to the small intervention introduced.

In the example of the observation sheet used by Gavin and the Secondary Mathematics Department, the recordings were simply a count of how many students appeared to be actively engaged vis-à-vis the lesson phase and activity. This data will not reveal details about who was involved or the actual nature of their involvement, however, the analysis of the overall patterns did show at what times and places the students, in general, seemed to be engaged (or not). In simple terms, for these teachers it showed that student engagement appeared to be high initially when the new activity was introduced, but after about 18 to 20 minutes it waned markedly, and this seemed common across all the classes. So, in response the teachers could modify their pedagogy and in the next cycle they overtly built in a teacher intervention at about the 15-minute mark to reset the students. The data also showed modest levels of engagement after about 30 minutes, and through discussing this evidence the teachers came to the conclusion that this related to students making varied progress – those who were seemingly succeeding maintained a high level of active participation, but those who were getting a little stuck perhaps 'gave up' and their enthusiasm dissipated. In response, the teachers also developed some enabling prompts for those who may have lost some momentum, and they planned to actively look out for the students who might need these from about the 25-minute mark of the lesson.

To support the teachers to more critically analyse their own and each other's classroom discussion practices (beyond more cursory commentary), Suzanne prepared a series of guide questions that acted as provocations for the ensuing professional dialogues. These questions were general in the beginning; for example, what have you been trying? how is it working? what differences are you noticing? what will you try next, why? As the teachers became more comfortable with viewing and critiquing each other's lessons, the professional questioning became more focused and fine-tuned. In response, Suzanne also developed her own questioning to have teachers focus on the student's responses; for example, what mathematical ideas and concepts are being communicated? How can these be developed and fine-tuned? Is the mathematics correct? How can we support students when they make an incorrect response? Reflection questions, like these, help to keeping the dialogues on the evidence at hand.

As a teacher herself, Suzanne knows teachers invest considerable time thinking about students and their actions in class, but this needs to be balanced with systematic reflection on teaching and its development. In this project, the challenge for Suzanne was to support teachers to learn efficient tools for analysing, reflecting on, responding to findings, and changing their own practice in a deliberate yet simple way. Here, teacher reflection stands at the corner between theory and practice. It is critical when it assists teachers make meaningful evaluations of their teaching, and time for allowing teachers to opportunities to align theory with practice or their *theory-of-practice-in-action*.

Supporting teachers to be reflective is evident when teachers recognise that they do not have all the answers, but continually work to improve themselves over time. Middle leading, like offered by Suzanne, is critical for supporting teachers to challenge their own practices and ways of thinking and to repeatedly engage in cycles of reflecting, planning, implementing, observing and reflecting once again. This process will provide opportunities for teachers to constantly learn from and respond to new situations and experiences by using the evidence to inform next steps for practice development in the action research cycle. From this perspective, reflective practice makes teachers responsive problem solvers who are constantly using evidence to adjust and learn from their own practice.

Connecting beyond the immediate community

Finally, as leaders of small professional communities of professionals, we think it is important to connect, share and collaborate with the wider profession beyond your immediate small professional group. Fundamentally, this is part of being in a profession, and it has 'inwards' and 'outwards' benefits. Inwardly, it can provide a sense of progress and achievement as you reflect on what you have collectively achieved, and outwardly it provides accounts and stories of what particular communities have done and achieved, and this can be a reflective 'touchstone' for other related groups and how they can proceed.

Case for study: working with other schools in a cluster

At the end of the first year of facilitating her school-based action research project at Riverbank Primary School, Suzanne's reputation for supporting teachers to consider their pedagogical approaches in terms of their capacity to make substantial changes to the kinds of questions they asked in mathematical discussions spread among schools in her local region. With encouragement from her principal Bob and Terry, the regional mathematics consultant, Suzanne became an instructional leader for a cluster of four schools (in close proximity to her). Although she maintained her classroom teaching allocation at Riverbank (3.5 days per week), her new role involved a day/week facilitating similar kinds of action research projects with selected teachers from the four schools. Part of her middle leading role included mentoring a lead teacher (Lisa) from her own school to take over the work she had begun at Riverbank. As Suzanne said, 'learning to lead takes time, I was provided the support and time, and goodwill and patience, to hone my facilitation skills so I think succession planning and mentoring others is an important part of school development'.

Initially Lisa worked with Suzanne in planning the cross-school sessions (based on the experiences as Riverbank) and shadowed her as she conducted the professional learning workshops, led the classroom walkthroughs and follow-up debrief sessions in the new schools. Building trust among the new teachers in the school was the key issue for Suzanne as she began working in their classrooms; her reputation was not enough. As a response, and with permission from Bob, to build relational trust Suzanne began to spend a lunchtime each week in each of the four cluster schools; as she said, 'my visibility and presence in the different staff rooms gave the teacher's time for informal chats and debriefing as they fine-tuned their thinking about their own development in a less pressured situation'. Flexibility and responsivity were important for working effectively in and across school settings.

Supported by school and district leadership, Lisa herself moved into a middle leading role. As Suzanne suggested, 'it is critical to also support the leading development of others'; Bob agreed, adding 'one of the important things about professional change is to sustain the focus, but at the same time make provisions for good operators to mentor others to lead'.

Case for study: reflected back and influencing others

After Gavin and the Secondary School Mathematics Department had engaged in the curriculum and pedagogical development through eight cycles of action research over the year, they had a final whole day department gathering to reflect on what they had learned, to celebrate their successes, and to begin thinking about what they wanted to do in the following year. Gavin brought out the baseline data that they had collected at the start of the year, and some other evidence sources they had used, to guide reflection and insights about the professional learning and curriculum development over the year. Some of the key developments that they noted included:

- a greater variety of teaching approaches had been employed in mathematics lessons;
- students learning was more to their previous learning and their 'lifeworlds';
- the approach to professional development had changed from 'attending courses' to school-based action research cycles, and no one wanted to go back to the previous practices;
- a more collegial and collective approach to mathematics education was developed in the school; and
- there were notable changes in classroom practice and the department 'culture'.

In the next year they flagged that they wanted to focus on developing a greater sense of appreciation for mathematics for its usefulness and its inherent beauty, and to start this they decided to spend their teacher day prior to classes starting actually 'doing' mathematics themselves.

On a broader school level, the changed practices and culture were noticed by others included other Department Heads and the Senior School Leadership Team. Formally, Gavin was asked to give a presentation to the whole staff at the beginning of the new year, and this occurred with the whole Department Team. Informally, the Head of Science and the Head of Arts also chatted with Gavin about how they had reformed their professional learning and curriculum development away from 'one day courses' towards a site-based, evidence-informed approach. From these discussions, these two departments began their own journey down this path, and also through the presentation to the whole staff, the Learning Support Team and some of the Physical Education staff started to try small aspects. When talking with their colleagues, Gavin and the other mathematics teachers would emphasise two main things: (1) it is a 'classroom out approach', rather than an 'imposed from above' approach, because it is responsive to the needs and conditions of the students and teachers concerned; and therefore, (2) there is no 'recipe about how to do it', and you have to find your own journey within the structure of the cycles. However, by sharing the story of their journey through the year, their account and their lived example brought about school-wide reform. Indeed, some two years later the school policies and guidelines were changed so that department-based action research was the 'way we operate around here'.

Conclusion

In this chapter we have used some extended case studies – one primary and one secondary – to exemplify how some of the principles and ideas that have been outlined in the previous chapters might unfold (be experienced) in practice. These are not intended to be recipes or templates about how middle leading happens; since, as we have made clear throughout, that middle leading needs to be developed in response to the actual conditions (needs and circumstances) and arrangements in each school site.

Theory-into-practice (TIPs): questions for reflection and discussion

So, as you have read and engaged with examples, we hope you have been able to reflect on your own middle leading in your own school context with your own professional community.

1 As a middle leader, what aspects of the case studies resonate with your leading context?

    a What issues or concerns seem familiar to you? What are different?
    b What middle leading practices might be useful in your site? How will you need to reconsider them for the particular conditions and arrangements of your school context?

2 Considering the key aspects outlined in this chapter:

    a How will you as a middle leader facilitate and manage a professional community of educators?
    b What might be some of your local considerations when thinking about the evidence needed to inform the curriculum and professional development of your team?
    c In what ways might you and your team be able to influence the practices of others?

Note

1 A professional team would include the teachers concerned, but it could also include teacher aides and other support staff.

References

DuFour, R. and Eaker, R. (1998). *Professional learning communities at work: best practices for enhancing student achievement.* Alexandria, VA: Association for Supervision and Curriculum Development.

Grootenboer, P. (2018). *The practices of school middle leadership: Leading professional learning.* Singapore: Springer.

Habermas, J. (1996). *Between facts and norms: Contributions to a discourse theory of law and democracy* (trans. Rehg, W.). Cambridge, Mass: MIT Press.

Hargreaves, A. (1994). *Changing teachers, changing times.* London: Cassell.

Kemmis, S., Wilkinson, J., Edwards-Groves, C., Hardy, I., Grootenboer, P. and Bristol, L. (2014). *Changing Practices, Changing Education.* Singapore: Springer Education.

Lave, J. and Wenger, E. (1991). *Situated learning: Legitimate peripheral participation.* Cambridge: Cambridge University Press.

Further reading

Kemmis, S., McTaggart, R. and Nixon, R. (2014). *The action research planner. Doing critical participatory action research.* Singapore: Springer.

7 Middle leading as a practice-changing practice

In this concluding chapter we consider middle leading, within the framework of practice architectures, to be a *practice-changing-practice*. With its broad purpose to facilitate school-based professional and curriculum development, middle leading changes leading, teaching, student learning, and school-based researching practices. In drawing these threads together, the chapter proposes that the new *gold standard* for professional learning is slowing it down and grounding the focus in the site – recognising and responding to its conditions and circumstances. Fundamentally, we propose that *Action-Oriented Professional Learning* is a useful way for middle leaders to conceptualise and facilitate the sort of professional development that can actually have an effect for students and schools. Importantly, at the end of this chapter (and book) we discuss how some of these ideas can, at times, be difficult to realise in the messiness and realities of school life – something that can be passed over in the stories of success that usually get told in books.

Action-Oriented Professional Learning: action, agency, and accomplishing educational change

Action in teacher professional learning is derived from a collaborative collegial workplace, built on a shared responsibility for learning and a culture through which people learn with and from each other (Kemmis *et al.*, 2014). An action-oriented professional learning approach to school-based professional development is based on the belief that when teachers, working collegially in small teams, are given opportunities to reflect critically and honestly on their practice, share their expertise with their colleagues, and so take more control of their own learning, they will not only increase their repertoire of effective teaching and assessment practices, but will also help to identify and resolve significant site-based challenges and issues.

Slowing it down – practising locally

Darling Hammond and colleagues (1995, 2009) have long cautioned against short term, episodic workshops disconnected from teachers' practices and concerns. Typically, such 'two-minute noodle' or 'drive-by' (Stein, Smith and Silver, 1999) approaches to professional learning are employed as a 'quick fixes' means of implementing systemic goals. Often, in particular, where the goal is to align with the key performance indicators required of bureaucrats; these we know are often well removed from the realities of teaching practice. Thus, for us, the efficacy in professional learning should not simply valorise what is short-term, readily visible, and easily measurable; it also must recognise, and perhaps even find merit in attempting to comprehend what is complex and problematic, what is uneven and unpredictable, what requires patience and tenacity. This means dealing with issues and practices that are often difficult to comprehend, or to find solutions for on your own.

Some significant features of accomplishing action and agency, slowly and assuredly, in educational change is through *Action-Oriented Professional Learning*; this includes:

- working collaboratively to focus on local issues and concerns to develop thoughtful solutions to local issues and concerns;
- improving systematically and slowly to develop sustainable and robust progress;
- negotiating and reflecting on evidence from practice; and
- acknowledging the personal and emotional dimension of educational change and development.

Localised collaboration

Action-oriented professional learning is site-based education development (Kemmis *et al.*, 2014). It is about learning and working in teams and it is the team and its dynamics, the experiences, expertise and learning (its challenged and successes) that each member brings to the team and its processes, that are central to action-oriented learning. Furthermore, it always begins with the teacher team's determination, commitment or even curiosity to deal with troublesome, urgent matters for which there may be unaware of any immediate solution, in their context. Thus, arguably the starting point for an action-oriented approach to learning may not only be the desire to improve existing practice, but may also be to develop deeper understandings of an issue for which there is no present practice. These principles of collaboration and 'site-basedness' have been replete throughout all the previous chapters of this book, and indeed, in our view they are essential dimensions of effective educational development.

Slow systematic development

Action-oriented professional learning begins with supporting teachers to develop their own theories of practice (previously we called this *a theory-of-practice-in-action),* to establish what is it they are setting out to accomplish, and some rationale as to why and how (Edwards-Groves ands Davidson, 2017). This step supports teachers keep their focus on what aspect of their practice they are attempting to develop. The process involves researching, investigating, studying, examining, and analysing, but the emphasis is not on researching other people's practices or consuming other peoples' research, but rather, investigating one's own practices in the company and support of others. Shared improvement in practice, thus, is achieved by teachers themselves reflecting on their daily work and asking, with the help of colleagues, in what ways might they do it more effectively. A key dimension of the process involves the systematic, consistent, and regular (and scheduled) opportunities to meet about, reflect on, and reframe practices over time. Of course, as would be clear through this book, the emphasis is on the educational practices that unfold in particular locations, and under site-based conditions.

Importantly, this involves beginning with *playing in the sandpit*. For sustainable change, teachers need *time* to practise new practices, try out new ideas, iron out problem spots, implement new programmes, adjust teaching to respond to student needs and circumstances. This means efficacy in middle leading requires 'giving and getting permission' to *play in the sandpit*. This time provides a necessary condition for securing more sustainable change; we say that this is a form of 'slow science'.

Negotiating and reflecting on evidence from practice

Action-oriented professional learning involves continuous iterative feedback from colleagues, teaching partners, and other team members. As will be clear from the preceding chapters, evidence-based development is critical to ensure that is based on understandings about what is actually happening in the site; this forms a vital component of action-oriented professional learning. Of course, care needs to be taken that the feed*up*-feed*back*-feed*forward* loop is designed to allow the teacher concerned to reflect on their own practice by increasing self-awareness about the impact and consequences of development and change, and of the conditions influencing progress *at the time*. Reflection on feedback enables teachers to generate and establish new courses of action that respond at the time without delay.

Personal dimension of change

Of course, any change can be fraught with all sorts of challenges and difficulties, and so it is important for middle leaders to *recognise risk*. Therefore, it obliges middle leaders and teachers to put at stake entrenched familiar practices, their own personal exploration of their practice and its underpinning values and beliefs. A supportive collegial learning environment is essential in this situation, and sometimes this can develop as a community of professionals start with something relatively simple, and as trust grows, deeper and more challenging issues can be examined. By comparison, consuming professional literature (or participating in prescribed programmes of development), case-based discussions, and theory-exchanges are lower-risk learning activities. Uncritical reporting to peers, unchallenged exhibition of classroom projects, or swapping of ideas and resources also carry relatively little risk. However, although the risks are perhaps lesser, often the capacity for significant growth is also diminished.

School-based action-oriented professional learning in practice

School-based action-oriented professional learning involves a small team of teachers in planning, action, observing, describing, recording, discussing, reflecting, evaluating and celebrating together. It will be obvious that this has a lot in common with action research, but perhaps here it provides a broader conception of the educational work in schools and its development. To this end, it might provide a useful framework for educational leaders in school. Rather than giving a long-winded discussion here, we have simply provided a fulsome list of the key features with some commentary.

1 *Teams of teachers*: a small group of colleagues (usually 6–8) teachers, with a shared responsibility and commitment for learning, form an action-oriented professional learning team to take effective action to address real learning and teaching challenges, opportunities or issues. Working in smaller teams:

   a *allows for more intense, serious, focused engagement of the team members;*
   b *builds relational trust;*
   c *supports confidentially among team members resulting in a greater willingness to share ideas and classroom experiences;*
   d *facilitates greater consistency and cohesion, since it is easier to gain agreement on purpose and direction in a small group;*
   e *provides more stability, as a small group is less likely to be affected by staff changes;*
   f *reduces or at least recognises complexity, in that it is easier to organise frequent regular team meetings; to share resources, etc.;*
   g *allows for more intensive support from the middle leader.*

2 *Project-based learning*: an action-oriented learning project addresses learning and teaching opportunities or challenges that are part of teacher's day-to-day practice, and for which there is no obvious, easily identified solutions.

3 *Participant direction-making*: teachers in the team decide on the area of inquiry and take control over their own learning. They decide on the goals, *set the pace*, choose the activities, judge the success of the project, and make decisions about future actions.

4 *Cycles of systematic inquiry*: action-oriented learning involves teachers in cycles of developing a professional learning action plan, implementing the plan, sharing and describing the effects of the action, and reflecting on and evaluating the action and the process. What teachers learn in each step of

the process informs decisions and action in subsequent steps and phases of the action-oriented learning cycles.

- a Observe, describe, record, discuss, and reflect upon the practice using a variety of strategies to gather evidence and describe practices including sharing observations, thoughts and ideas, interviews, focus group discussions, journals or learning logs, portfolios, video scenarios, photographs, and annotated student work samples.
- b *Reflecting* is a critical part of the process as a tool for professional learning. It assists teachers to notice, name, and reframe practices in terms of sayings, doings, and relatings. It involves teachers considering not only what they are doing in the classroom, but also, why they are doing it. It involves review, analysis, and interpretation of evidence and experience to make meaning, on-balance judgments and decisions about future action. Tips for reflection:

    i Identify beliefs and assumptions that underpin key practices, the actions and decisions taken.
    ii Ask: 'what if we were to....?' To test alternative approaches.
    iii Move beyond first thoughts or taken-for-granted meanings and explanations.
    iv Challenge dominant or popular ideas with alternatives.
    v Attempt to frame or reframe a particular teaching experience or assessment task.
    vi Explore connections between events, feelings, actions and experiences.
    vii Attempt to forecast intended and unintended consequences of particular actions.
    viii Identify and make overt actions and reactions in classroom 'bumpy moments'.
    ix Identify gaps in terms of what is known and unknown about a particular topic.
    x Pose questions that need to be addressed by the team.

5 *Learning Partnerships*: school-based action learning teams often form partnerships with bodies external to the school, such as professional associations, universities, and other tertiary institutions and consultants. They do this to access existing experiences in their field and to obtain an outside perspective on their work and learning.

Leading action-oriented professional learning

In this final section on action-oriented professional learning, we focus on the role and practices of the middle leader as a facilitator, manager, and director. This form of meaningful professional learning hands more control of learning to the learner (i.e. the teachers). It requires teachers to critically reflect on, respond to, and review learning in a focused, but more importantly, analytic way. So, a key part of the middle leader's role is to work with a structure that allows time and practices for this to happen. Middle leaders need to plan for and provide a range of opportunities for teachers to routinely respond to their professional learning and engage in focused reflection and review that, over time, enables them to develop critical thinking as a habit of their professional learning. Thus, professional learning needs to be filled with dialogic activities that count towards maximising learning for all.

Planning the session

When planning 'what to do in the session', it is necessary for middle leaders to consider the activities, strategies, and tasks that facilitate action. It is useful to prepare 'jump start' activities to orient the teachers, and to provide a range of engaging approaches to the PL that will enable them to revisit the learning through self-reflection, response, review, and summary. In planning meaningful learning experiences middle leaders need to consider a range of interactive strategies that form the basis of dialogic ways of working (Appendix 2 and 6 provides a range of strategies that can be used or adapted).

Preparing teachers for learning: teachers should not dive in to the new agenda without some kind of preparation. 'Jump-start' strategies that prepare the learning path assist teachers to *tune in* the professional learning programme by activating and focusing thinking applicable to new learning. Explicit connection-making assists in identifying relevant prior skills and knowledge about the topic for learning and are important because they help to establish the professional learning purposes; the rationale; and the relationship to the site-based conditions, needs and circumstances of the school, community, and students. Strategies that ignite focused thinking and connection-making prevents learners from 'going in cold' by preparing the path for purposeful learning by:

- giving the responsive facilitator, the middle leader, the chance to climb inside the learner's mind to discover what is already known so that the session can build onto current understandings and knowledge;
- turning minds on to the learning assists learners to engage in topical thinking; and
- providing *hooks* upon which the learner can hang new learning on in the evolving process of learning.

Revisit learning through self-reflection, response, review and summary: reflective experiences form essential components of quality and efficacy in professional learning and teaching change. Focused reflection enables critical time for teachers to illuminate what is at the forefront of their thinking (the messages they are bringing to and taking away from the sessions). This part of a session helps to inform teachers in their future planning for actions to be taken in their action research; and provide further opportunities to consolidate and tease out the details of the learning. Over the period of the professional learning project, the middle leader might need to consider the following issues and procedures in order to facilitate maximum support.

> This process will prompt and support teachers to learn more about reasons for their own actions, as well as learn more about the process of self-reflection.
> (adapted from Edwards-Groves, 2003)
>
> - Negotiate specific details and time-lines with individual teachers. Ensure a framework or schedule is in place to facilitate teacher commitment.
> - Review lessons or observation notes with teachers to provide critical (positive) feedback and comment.
> - Challenge teachers in a way that maintains the critical points of change as the project focus.
> - It is important to be vigilant in addressing the negotiated aspects of change. Therefore, the orientation to the main categories for change remains primary (e.g. don't get too distracted by 'red-herring' or divergent talk about other matters like resources, furniture arrangements, school routines, timetables, etc.).
> - Provide a sounding board against which teacher could try out ideas.
> - Reflect on the process and change focus in a journal or notebook. Encourage the teacher to note personal observations including anecdotal field notes, evaluations, and points for further development and discussion. The journal is particularly important for helping teachers to work in *self-paced* ways as it provides an on-going record of the process of change and development.
> - Provide regular support though *informal* discussions, observations, teacher comments, and other collected information related to the main themes provides systematic support. It can be shared, discussed, recorded, evaluated, and acted upon on a daily basis as a part of a regular formative review. This sequence provides on-going monitoring and evaluation for participating teachers and can form the basis of a review of progress and a springboard upon which the structure of consequent lessons can be formed. Additionally, these discussions are an opportunity for teacher self-assessment. Review can be based on these questions: *What did you try? What worked well? Why? What didn't work well? Why? What will be tried/worked on in the next lesson?*
> - Encourage teachers to contact you at any stage.

Focused reflection and review involve guiding teacher thinking and action before, during and at the end of each of the learning sessions enabling teachers to integrate, consolidate, apply and connect to what is newly learnt.

Leading change – beyond nice stories and embracing the messiness

One of the things we notice in many accounts of school-based action research development is that they appear to be relatively smooth and trouble-free; these are often reported as experiences that 'always' result in positive and sustainable outcomes. These nice stories appear wonderful, but we know from working across many school sites and districts across the world that it is not that simple or straight-forward – school-based educational development is messy and complex! It is for this reason that middle leaders are crucial for leading and facilitating curriculum and professional development, because they work in the hectic milieu in and around classrooms, and can appreciate the convoluted nature of educational practice and change. Of course, the factors and issues that make educational development and action research 'messy' are site-based. Nevertheless, some of the common ones we have seen relate to:

- finding quality time;
- being able to step aside from the regular business and routines of school life;
- dealing with significant issues or concerns; and
- working with reluctant staff.

Of course, this is not an exhaustive list, and we have addressed some of these issues in previous chapters (e.g. time and stepping aside from school routines).

Addressing substantial issues

We have read and heard many accounts of school-based development projects, and it seems to us that almost all of these report on successful projects that address and resolve significant issues. However, we have also worked in schools (as teachers, middle leaders, and supporters of school initiatives) and we know that often the focus of the 'project' is relatively simple and of limited significance, and the educational gains are regularly modest. Sometimes the teacher's action research plan is not appropriate (i.e. does not respond to students' needs or circumstances) or might even reflect or generate 'mis-information' or 'half-formed ideas'. Does the middle leader simply acquiesce? (Glickman, 2002). This is a pragmatic, but substantial, question for the middle leader; what is right to do under such circumstances? In such a case, the middle leader (knowing they also need to accept the teacher's rights and responsibilities for their own practice and learning) also has the right and the responsibility to explain his or her misgivings about the plan and ask for reconsideration, and to offer alternatives or advice (Davidson and Edwards-Groves, 2019; Glickman, 2002). This is a delicate matter (Davidson and Edwards-Groves, 2019); and can leave those involved feeling disillusioned and deflated. Middle leaders should not take this to heart, since the complexity and struggle of change is often both confronting and time consuming for teachers; keep it professional not personal.

While we can understand and empathise with this situation, we think that it is important that middle leaders take the long view of school-based development. Invariably when initiating this sort of approach, there are a range of factors that can limit progress, and it takes time for new ways of working to be established, accepted, and enacted. Therefore, when starting it is often prudent to begin with an issue or focus that is relatively simple and does not involve too much 'risk'. This enables teachers to take the time and space required to begin to feel comfortable working and sharing together, and engaging in practices like classroom observations for evidence collection. If teachers experience success and comfort in this somewhat rudimentary form of action-oriented professional learning, then they are more likely to engage in deeper and more challenging concerns in subsequent iterations. Of course, these gains can only be realised if the shift towards site based educational development becomes the standard way of operating for the group of teachers. This view opens up learning stance not restricted by the timeframe of a contained 'project', that once 'done' the staff move onto the next initiative or project. We would go so far as to say that even if it is just a one-year project or initiative, then it probably is not worth the effort, as the significant gains are often only realised in the fulness of time.

Reluctant staff

Another confounding factor in action-oriented professional learning approach can be staff who are reluctant to be involved, or who perhaps engage in a perfunctory manner. These can include experienced teachers who have taught for many years and are somewhat 'set in their ways', teachers with very fixed ideas about pedagogy, or new teachers who are pre-occupied with initial matters like classroom management, accreditation for registration, and understanding school systems. Sometimes the initial enthusiasm gives way to confusion and reluctance and the abandonment of the commitment to the initiative when reform and transformation is slower than expected, or is unpredictable or undesirable. Sometimes resistance exists on the surface, true interest or vulnerability lies disguised beneath an isolationist mirage or a veil of excuses or bravado or unarticulated hopes. Whatever the case, it is clear that these staff members will make a site-based professional learning approach more challenging, and their involvement will detract from the possibilities for effective development. Given the diverse nature of 'reluctance' or 'resistance', there is not a simple solution to how this dilemma can be rectified.

Under such conditions, however, it is important for the middle leader to adopt a *listening stance*. This involves showing attention to each individual teacher by *listening* empathically to the issues and problems they are facing, and acknowledging the 'said' frustrations as they are heard. In any case, listening first forms a critical part of moving towards potential solutions. The next step, suggested by Glickman (2002) involves *encouraging* the teacher to break down the problem further, to analyse it collaboratively. *Clarifying* follows; here the middle leader clarifies the teacher's issue/problem through paraphrasing, revoicing and questioning. At this point the middle leader might offer advice, alternative perspectives or other suggestions if the teacher asks. Critically, to move towards *problem solving*, the process should finish with collaborative *decision-making* about what to do. Nevertheless, some general considerations include: (1) voluntary 'opt-in' participation; (2) a professional approach; (3) managing and facilitating the conditions and arrangements; and (4) starting with the long-term in mind.

An early issue that a middle leader will need to consider is whether an action-oriented professional learning approach is compulsory for all in the team or group concerned. This can be a vexed point, because it is ideal to have all members of a teaching team engaging together and collaboratively, but compulsion does not engender fulsome participation or shared commitment, so there is not a clear 'answer'. In the past, we have tended to see involvement as voluntary, as we saw the gains from enthusiastic and whole-hearted participation as important and significant. The goal then is, once others see how professional rewarding and effective the 'new' approach is, then they may be more likely to want to be involved, and therefore, the invitation to participate must always be open.

Second, and relatedly, the approach to professional learning and development we have proposed in this book really is only effective with teachers who are professional in the teaching practice. By this, we mean that it is not a way to fix or remediate an incompetent teacher. We appreciate that incompetent teachers are few and far between, and so this may well not be an issue in most schools, but the fundamental principle of a *professional* learning is that it requires the teachers involved to be and to practise in a professional manner – indeed, inquiring into and developing one's own practice is a fundamental characteristic of a professional.

To facilitate meaningful and on-going commitment to an action-oriented professional learning approach will require the middle leader to be thoughtful and careful in managing the practice architectures that enable and constrain it. This has already been discussed in detail in previous chapters, but perhaps here all that is needed is a reminder that often teachers are willing to engage in site-based professional and curriculum development, but the pressures and busy tasks of school life can squeeze out the available quality time, and sap the participants energy and enthusiasm, resulting in reluctant engagement. Therefore, managing the professional time of staff, and being a mediator between the demands from senior management can be a critical role for the middle leader as they lead and facilitate meaningful and effective teacher engagement and participation.

Finally, in the same vein as we concluded the last section, we think it is important to a take-term view of action-oriented professional learning, and this means that there is no need to necessarily focus on big significant issues at the start. It is likely that teachers will be less reluctant to be involved if the initially the approach seems manageable, doable, and non-threatening. Then, with success, confidence and increasing trust, more substantial issues can be broached as teachers are more invested and committed to the 'way of being' a learning teacher.

Conclusion

As we draw this chapter and book to a close, we want to re-emphasise that we see the middle leader as the crucial agent in leading school-based curriculum and pedagogical development, and throughout we have tried to provide robust ideas and tools to help them in this role. Specifically, in this chapter all these ideas have been drawn together by focusing on *action-oriented professional learning* – a concept and framework that helps middle leaders to consider and organise the professional and curriculum development in their site. This final chapter was concluded with some discussion of some of the pragmatic issues that can arise in the actual practice of middle leading in the hustle and bustle of school life. While it was not our intention to finish on a low note with 'possible problems', we did want to situate the ideas presented with an appreciation for the realistic life of teachers and schools. That said, we are positive about the important educational impact that middle leaders can uniquely have in school sites, and so we see the investment in supporting the significant leadership work they do as crucial.

Theory-into-practice (TIPs): questions for reflection and discussion

In practical ways, middle leaders need to lead teachers into focused reflective discussion and activity. Drawing on the interactive strategies and focused guide questions (available Appendix 6), consider the particular strategies that support the teachers in the professional learning team to:

i *state the obvious* – involving review talk, thinking, and activity – beginning from what is known coming into the session, what details, facts, experiences, etc.

ii *go beyond the obvious* – involving reflective talk thinking and activity – Where does it fit? How does it fit? What does this mean?

iii *establish connections* – involving reflective talk, thinking, and activity – What I already know? How does this take my learning further? Why we learnt this? Where does it take me? What else does it relate to what I know about/would like to know about?

iv *express values* – involving response talk, thinking, and activity – How do I respond to this? – What are my attitudes to this? How do I react to it? How do I feel? What are other points of view?

v *examine implications* – involving reflective and response talk, thinking, and activity – Now I know this what else can I do? Where to from here? What is the impact on others?

vi *reflect critically on responses and learning processes* – involving reflective talk, thinking and activity – How did I go? How did I learn this? What is easy? What remains a challenge? Where to from here? Are there gaps?

Use these as a basis for planning an upcoming session with your colleagues. Reflect yourself on how the different phases of reflective talk facilitated teacher dialogue. What happened?

References

Darling-Hammond, L. and McLaughlin, M. W. (1995). 'Policies that support professional development in an era of reform', *Phi Delta Kappan*, 76(8), 597–604.

Darling Hammond, L. and Richardson, N. (2009). 'Research Review/Teacher Learning: What Matters?', *How Teachers Learn*, 66(5), 46–53.

Davidson, C. and Edwards-Groves, C. (2019). 'Managing the delicate matter of advice giving: Accomplishing communicative space in Critical Participatory Action Research', *Educational Action Research Journal*. https://doi.org/10.1080/09650792.2018.1559744.

Edwards-Groves, C. (2003). *On Task: Focused Literacy Learning*. Newtown, Sydney, NSW: Primary English Teaching Association Australia (PETAA).

Edwards-Groves, C. and Davidson, C. (2017). *Becoming a Meaning Maker: Talk and Interaction in the Dialogic Classroom*. Newtown, Sydney, NSW: Primary English Teaching Association Australia (PETAA).

Glickman, C. (2002). *Leadership for Learning: How to Help Teachers Succeed*. Alexandria, VA, US: ASCD.

Kemmis, S., Wilkinson, J., Edwards-Groves, C., Hardy, I., Grootenboer, P. and Bristol, L. (2014). *Changing Practices, Changing Education*. Singapore: Springer Education.

Stein, M. K., Smith, M. S. and Silver, E. A. (1999). 'The development of professional developers: Learning to assist teachers in new settings in new ways', *Harvard Educational Review*, 69(3), 237–269.

Further reading

This next set of readings are intended for those who might like to explore the issue of middle leading, professional learning, and action research in more depth (perhaps for further study).

Carr, W. and Kemmis, S. (1986). *Becoming critical: education, knowledge and action research*. Warum Ponds, Victoria: Deakin University Press.

Crane, A. and De Nobile, J. (2014). 'Year coordinators as middle-leaders in independent girls' schools: Their role and accountability', *Leading & Managing*, 20(1), 80–92.

Cresswell, J. W. (2008). *Educational research: planning, conducting and evaluating quantitative and qualitative research*, 3rd edition. Upper Saddle River, New Jersey: Pearson.

De Nobile, J. (2014). 'Examining middle level leadership in schools using a multi-role framework'. Paper presented at 'Passion & Purpose: Setting the Learning Agenda', Australian Council for Educational Leaders National Conference, Melbourne, 1–3 October 2014.

De Nobile, J. (2016). 'Measuring middle level leadership: The development of the middle leadership roles questionnaire'. Paper presented at 'Leadership with Insight & Innovation: Setting the Learning Agenda', Australian Council for Educational Leaders National Conference, Melbourne, 28–30 September 2016.

De Nobile, J. (2017). 'Towards a theoretical model of middle leadership in schools', *School Leadership & Management*, 38(4), 395–416.

De Nobile, J. and Ridden, P. (2014). 'Middle leaders in schools: Who are they and what do they do?', *Australian Educational Leader*, 36(2), 22–25.

Dewey, J. (1938). *Logic: the theory of inquiry*. New York: Holt, Rinehart & Winston.

Dewey, J. (1938, 1998). *Experience & Education: 60th anniversary edition*. New York: Kappa Delta Pi.

Dick, B. (2011). 'Action Research literature 2008–2010', *Action Research*, 9(2).

Edwards-Groves, C. and Rönnerman, K. (2013). 'Generating leading practices through professional learning', *Professional Development in Education*, 39(1), 122–140.

Edwards-Groves, C., Grootenboer, P. and Rönnerman, K. (2016). 'Facilitating a culture of relational trust in school-based action research: Recognising the role of middle leaders'. *Educational Action Research*, 24(3). doi:10.1080/09650792.2015.1131175.

Edwards-Groves, C., Grootenboer, P. and Rönnerman, K (2018). 'Middle Leading: Examining the Practice Architectures of Leading Sustainable Site-based Practice Development in Schools'. American Educational Research Association Conference (AERA), New York, April 2018.

Edwards-Groves, C., Grootenboer, P. and Attard, C. (2019). 'Conceptualising Three Core Practices for Leading Site-based Educational Development in Schools: A Practice Architectures Perspective'. American Educational Research Association Conference (AERA), Toronto, April 2019.

Edwards-Groves, C., Grootenboer, P., Hardy, I. and Rönnerman, K. (2018). 'Driving change from 'the middle': middle leading for site based educational development', *School Leadership & Management*. doi:10.1080/13632434.2018.1525700.

Grootenboer, P. and Larkin, K. (2019). 'Middle leading small-scale school projects', *International Journal of Educational Management*. doi:10.1108/IJEM-12-2018-0407.

Grootenboer, P., Edwards-Groves and Rönnerman, K. (2014). 'Leading practice development: Voices from the middle', *Professional Development in Education*, 41(3), 508–526.

Grootenboer, P., Edwards-Groves, C. and Rönnerman, K. (2015). The practice of middle leading in mathematics education. In M. Marshman, V. Geiger and A. Bennison (Eds), *Mathematics education in the margins* (Proceedings of the 38th annual conference of the Mathematics Education Research Group of Australasia) (pp. 277–284). Sunshine Coast: MERGA.

Grootenboer, P., Rönnerman, K. and Edwards-Groves, C. (2017). Leading from the Middle: A Praxis-Oriented Practice. In P. Grootenboer, C. Edwards-Groves and S. Choy (Eds), *Practice Theory Perspectives on Pedagogy and Education: Praxis, diversity and contestation* (pp. 243–263). Singapore: Springer.

Kemmis, S. (2011). A self-reflective practitioner and a new definition of critical participatory action research. In N. Mockler and J. Sachs (Eds), *Rethinking educational practice through reflexive inquiry: an introduction*. Dordrecht, Netherlands: Springer.

Kemmis, S. and McTaggart, R. (1988). *The action research planner*. Warum Ponds, Victoria: Deakin University Press.

Rönnerman, K. (2015). 'The Importance of Generating Middle Leading through Action research for Collaborative Learning', *LEARNing Landscapes*, 8(2), 33–39. E-journal www.learninglandscapes.ca/current-issue.

Rönnerman, K. and Olin, A. (2014). Research Circles – Constructing a Space for Elaborating on being a Teacher Leader in Preschools. In K. Rönnerman and P. Salo (Eds), *Lost in Practice: Transforming Nordic Educational Action Research* (pp. 95–112). Rotterdam: Sense Publishers.

Rönnerman, K., Edwards-Groves, C. and Grootenboer, P. (2014). 'Opening up communicative spaces in early childhood education through middle leadership'. Paper presented at the conference, Educational Leadership in transition–the Global Perspective. Uppsala, 5–6 November 2014. http://int.blasenhus.uu.se/papersELTGP/KRO637.pdf.

Rönnerman, K., Edwards-Groves, C. and Grootenboer, P. (2015). 'Opening up communicative spaces for discussion 'quality practices' in early childhood education through middle leadership', *Nordic Journal of Studies in Educational Policy*. http://dx.doi.org/10.3402/nstep.v1.30098.

Rönnerman, K., Edwards-Groves, C. and Grootenboer, P. (2017). 'Action research generates middle leading for professional learning of others'. Paper presented in Collaborative Action Research Network (CARN), Crete, Greece, November 2017.

Rönnerman, K., Edwards-Groves, C. and Grootenboer, P. (2018). *Att leda från mitten – lärare driver professionell utveckling* [Leading from the middle – Teachers driving professional development]. Stockholm: Lärarförlaget.

Rönnerman, K., Grootenboer, P. and Edwards-Groves, C. (2017). 'The Practice Architectures of Middle Leading in Early Childhood Education', *International Journal of Child Care and Education Policy*, 11(8). doi:10.1186/s40723–40017–0032-z.

Ruddock, J. and Hopkins, D. (1985). *Research as a basis for teaching: readings from the work of Lawrence Stenhouse*. London: Heinemann.

Schon, D. (1987). *Educating the Reflective Practitioner*. San Francisco: Jossey Bass.

Appendix 1: Facilitating teacher reflection: questions and strategies

Focused critical teacher reflection stands at the corner between theory and practice. It illuminates the details of teaching and learning practices as teachers consider successes and challenges about their practice both at the micro level (the minute-by-minute unfolding of a lesson) and the macro level (in planning, resourcing and enacting teaching, or at the policy and curriculum level). Reflective teachers constantly learn from, and respond to, new situations, knowledge and experiences. True reflective practice makes teachers responsive problem solvers who are constantly adjusting and refining their practice according to situations, subject areas and the student groups. Middle leaders can facilitate a focus on practice through modelling and prompting teacher reflection by encouraging them to critically examine their own lesson practices.

The following strategies (adapted from Edwards-Groves, 2003) can assist middle leaders to support teachers examine and critically reflect on their own lessons. To fine-tune their current practice, teachers should be encouraged to select those strategies that suit their circumstances. Each strategy should lead to deliberate, authentic action. They can be used as a springboard for individual reflection or for collaborative professional learning dialogues; and build onto many of the ideas found across this book.

Reflective practice: illuminating teaching and learning

The following reflective practices provide a collection of suggested approaches that teachers may find useful for shedding light on, building individual competence and developing their practice.

Teach and look back

Encourage the teachers to take time to ask self-reflection questions about their lesson practices: *What worked? What didn't? How do you know? What gave you that idea? What would you do differently next time? What will you try tomorrow? Did you do a better job on the aspect that you are trying to improve?* (e.g. remembering to incorporate meaningful review, allowing wait time, asking inferential type questions rather than predominantly literal, calling on students to articulate their learning, asking students for justification or clarification). *Did you allow the students to build onto their original ideas or onto each other's ideas?*

Video-recording or audio-recording lessons

Video- or audio- recording their own lessons can provide teachers with sometimes startling insights into their practice. Some teachers will say 'Oh, I could never do that!', but you are there to say 'Yes you can!'. Say, '*Once you get past the way you look and the way you sound, tapes offer rich information about your teaching practices. In particular, they reveal what your students hear to be the focal point of the lesson – how they talk about and think about their learning. They show aspects of teaching that cannot be gauged simply by recalling the lesson.*' Reflecting on recordings take the focus of teacher reflection to a new level.

Learning logs – journaling – blogging

> *Noticing and naming practices are one important step towards reframing and transforming practices.*
>
> (Edwards-Groves and Davidson, 2017)

Focused writing is a powerful tool for reflective learning and development; but is one that is often dispreferred by many teachers. By keeping a daily/weekly reflection log or diary, teachers can learn a great deal about themselves as a teacher, and about their student learning processes. Learning logs also help teachers to focus on themselves as learners by documenting small *noticings* and changes over time. Furthermore, writing helps teachers to discover gaps in their thinking, learning and knowledge (Dillon, 2000). Note: since many teachers find it hard to or are resistant to writing and journaling – find innovative ways like blogging, contributing to a shared staff noticeboard – to support the process.

Peers' observation and reflection

One of the best resources available to a teacher is another teacher – the middle leader, a colleague from their own school or teaching team, a teacher from a learning network, a consultant or other professional peer. Be focused in the observation and debriefing. To begin, help the teacher through:

1. *Pre-observation*: Identify a particular aspect of the teaching on which they would like to concentrate. For example, the teacher might be trying to improve their classroom discussions, or they might want to reduce the fragmentation of learning by reducing incidental talk, or add depth to your questioning by including more open-ended questions, or develop consistency in your use of wait time.
2. *Observation*: Take notes related to the established focus.

3   *Debrief meeting*: It is critical that the observation session is followed by a debriefing session that allows you and the teacher to share perceptions and evaluations of the lesson in relation to the focus (Friel, 1997). Say to the teacher 'Don't try to focus on everything at once: be kind to yourself and choose one main category at a time for change or refinement.'

The dialogue conference: round robin reflection and collegial conversations

The dialogue conference comprised of focused conversations around professional issues (of teaching, student learning) that matter to individuals or are a specific focus of teacher individual action research projects provides a shared space for building collegiality and overcoming challenges as a group. This reflection strategy enables all participants equal time to share an aspect of their learning they are challenged by, and enables the 'collective wisdom' to be made public. It also assists teachers to *notice, name and reframe* their thinking as they listen to the ideas of others.

Preparation: Before the collegial sharing day/meeting every participating teacher develops one PowerPoint slide that encompasses an aspect of their action research learning they have *noticed* or are interested in with a particular focus on a success, and a challenge or a problem they face with the 'next steps' in their learning project. This slide forms a provocation and stimulation for conducting focused professional learning conversations. These can be combined to develop a 'whole school' or 'team' brief.

In the meeting, each teacher will then talk to their slide (see the information below); designate a scribe and timekeeper for each round (this task can be shared around the group).

Protocol for each sharing round (20 minutes/teacher):

- (five mins) *Noticing and naming*: the teacher shares her/ his slide and articulates or *names their project and their noticings*, sharing the success, and then articulates the challenge or a problem they are attempting to address in their own inquiry project or action research.
- (two mins) *Thinking, connecting, and critiquing*: each other individual member then thinks and writes feedback using *post-its* to *connect* to the challenge or the problem posed, *extend* thinking about what was heard, and/or *challenge* the thinking about the practice.
- (10 mins) *The collaborative analytic dialogue*: the group engages in dialogue about the issue and feedback. Clarifying or probing questions may be asked, challenges posed, etc. The teacher takes notes.
- (three mins) *Towards reframing*: the teacher then responds to share how the group's comments and questions *extended* and/or *challenged* her or his thinking; a designated scribe (also the time keeper) creates extra *post-its* as necessary.

Summary and synthesis format (time permitting):

- (five mins) The middle leader (or a nominated scribe) reviews the broad themes of problems and challenges generated in the sessions, using the post-it notes as a stimulus for collating the ideas and propositions.
- (10 mins) Group dialogues about where there may be overlap across themes and suggests merger of some ideas into 3–5 common challenges.

Observe other teachers

Arrange for teachers to observe a willing colleague who is known to be an effective teacher or has been working on a similar strategy. Encourage teachers to think about the attributes they are trying to improve and focus the observations on these; watching specifically for the things that are working well. How is the teacher organising the students for learning? What grouping structures are in place? What can be taken back to other classrooms to try tomorrow? Allow time after the observation for debriefing in a focused reflection and discussion session.

Teacher self-reflection questions

The questions below are provided to guide focused teacher reflection. It is not necessary to address every question. Rather, middle leaders should add or adapt questions to meet individual purposes and professional learning goals of individual teachers or teaching teams.

Ask teachers to ask themselves: What counts in my lessons? Do I accomplish what I set out to teach? How do I know? Is it evident in the talk of the classroom?

Teacher lesson talk

- How am I focusing the students at the beginning of the lessons?
- How do I introduce the main learning goals of the lesson? Is the new learning made explicit? Do I share the specific nature of the learning task, along with its rationale, its value to students' learning and its relevance to their lives?
- How do I use assessment information to guide my practice? Do I plan learning opportunities that have clear and well-defined purposes?
- Do I do most of the talking?
- Do I explicitly teach students to listen to each other? To collaborate? To cooperate?
- To what extent do I use the repertoire of dialogic pedagogies in my practice? Do I provide opportunities and time for students to:
  - sustain their thinking;
  - extend and deepen their thinking;

- respectfully challenge the ideas and opinions of others;
- think through and formulate ideas and opinions;
- ask different kinds of questions;
- control the learning dialogue with peers;
- give learning focused responses;
- reflect on and review learning;
- collaborate and cooperate;
- listen actively;
- practise and rehearse ideas;
- articulate thoughts, ideas and opinions and rephrase if necessary;
- give others time to think;
- respond with and engage with the reasoning of others;
- come to consensus;
- give and receive feedback respectfully;
- narrate; explain; instruct, receive, act and build upon answers; analyse and solve problems; speculate and imagine; explore and evaluate ideas; negotiate; discuss, argue, reason and justify.

- Does the lesson talk ensure that students are aware of what it is they will be expected to demonstrate to show achievement of the task?
- Is the learning focus maintained throughout the lesson?
- Does my lesson talk respond authentically to students' learning needs in a way that supports and extends their learning?
- Do I scaffold the learner by demonstrating and modelling new processes, concepts and knowledge?
- Do I provide explicit feedback that links students' responses and performance to the lesson goals?
- Do I allow time at the lesson conclusion to reconnect students to their learning — that is, to reflect on, reformulate or articulate their learning?
- What 'take-home messages' are students left with as a result of this lesson?
- Am I allowing lesson time for purposeful reflection and review?
- Am I using wait time before and after I receive responses to questions?
- Am I exploring alternative strategies and ideas posed by different students?
- Am I encouraging productive thinking and on-task talk?
- Is there evidence of take-up?

Student lesson talk

- What do my students talk about?
- Do students ask questions? What kinds of questions are my students asking?
- Are my students talking with each other — challenging, justifying, debating?
- Are my students listening to each other?
- Are my students willing to take risks? Like what?

Appendix 1

- Are my students taking time to think about the problem, question, idea?
- Can my students build onto each other's ideas?
- Are my students able to explain their ideas clearly and precisely?
- Are my students able to reflect on their learning and identify: What was hard? What was easy? What worked? What didn't? What they liked? What they didn't like?
- How are they relating to one another?
- Can my students:

    - Sustain their thinking?
    - Extend and deepen their thinking?
    - Respectfully challenge the ideas and opinions of others?
    - Think through and formulate ideas and opinions?
    - Ask different kinds of questions?
    - Control the learning dialogue with peers?
    - Give learning focused responses?
    - Reflect on and review learning?
    - Collaborate and cooperate?
    - Listen actively?
    - Practise and rehearse ideas?
    - Articulate thoughts, ideas and opinions and rephrase if necessary?
    - Give others time to think?
    - Respond with and engage with the reasoning of others?
    - Come to consensus?
    - Give and receive feedback respectfully?
    - Narrate; explain; instruct, receive, act and build upon answers; analyse and solve problems; speculate and imagine; explore and evaluate ideas; negotiate; discuss, argue, reason and justify?

Resources and tools for learning

- Am I making appropriate use of technology? For a range of purposes?
- Do I encourage the use of various tools, modes and forms to represent and communicate ideas?
- Is a range of texts used for a wide range of purposes? For stimulus and models? For interest and learning?

The learning environment

- Is the physical environment arranged to facilitate discussion?
- Is the environment stimulating and interesting?
- Is the environment continually changing to reflect current learning?
- Are students encouraged to show respect for, listen to and respond to other students?

References

Dillon, D. (2000). *Kids insight: Reconsidering how to meet the literacy needs of all students*. Newark, DE: International Reading Association.

Edwards-Groves, C. (2003). On-task thinking: Reflective teaching and learning. *On Task: focused literacy learning*. Newtown, Sydney, NSW: Primary English Teaching Association Australia (PETAA).

Edwards-Groves, C. and Davidson, C. (2017). *Becoming a Meaning Maker: Talk and Interaction in the Dialogic Classroom*. Newtown, Sydney, NSW: Primary English Teaching Association Australia (PETAA).

Friel, S. (Ed.) (1997). 'The role of reflection in teaching: do you need to change your teaching practices?', *Arithmetic Teacher*. National Council of Teachers of Mathematics.

Appendix 2: Interactive strategies for facilitating focused reflection, rich discussion, and critical thinking

Designing engaging dialogic professional learning involves utilising a range of interactive of approaches that provide opportunities for reflective teaching and learning. The following strategies (adapted from Edwards-Groves, 2003) can be used before, during and after a session to facilitate reflective dialogue.

Poster trail

A learner reflection strategy. On poster-sized paper, leaders post up around the room a series (suggest 3–6) of pertinent concepts, questions, summary points or key ideas from the lesson or from the previous lesson and have in readiness Post-it notes and pens. Teacher learners (individually or in learning teams) move around the 'carousel' to each poster and spend a small amount of set time at each station brainstorming/responding to/questioning the points or statements written. If groups are used a designated 'recorder' rotates with the group to record the ideas or question generated.

Stop and ask time

Used to develop effective questioning and thinking skills and to encourage active listening among learners. At strategic points during a session, teacher learners are asked to stop and write down a question (on a post it or in their note books) about the point, topic or issue.

Hit the pause button

At any point during a PL session, pause the flow of discussion/instruction by calling 'pause button'. A reflective question is posed by the leader (or designated participant). A brief discussion follows and groups are asked to respond. The purpose is to allow learners to process information, deepen responses and elaborate on ideas or opinions. It allows learners time to make connections and perceive relevancy to their own lives, learning, practices, development focus. Possible prompt questions could include: what is happening here? what are the core issues we are discussing? why is this concept important to our lives? how does what we are talking about connect with other experiences or other issues from previous sessions?

Whip around

A brief 'whip around' where each person in a small group contributes one idea or sentence. This process is designed upon the previous thought or to add a further dimension to the thinking process. Can be used at the beginning or end of a session, or after a discussion to focus the thinking in a critical way.

Piggybacking

This strategy is similar to the WHIP (see above), but each person PIGGY-BACKS on the response of the previous speaker by saying 'I agree (or disagree) that……,' or 'to add on to that.'. Each responder provides a reason, a rationale, an example or justification for their comment. Comments may be recorded to build the record of ideas.

Huddle

Like a football huddle, groups of learners join together to answer questions, compare ideas, collate ideas, make conclusions. Speed is a factor and all learners contribute. This strategy can be used widely and is particularly useful when a series of points or questions need to be worked through quickly, with input from the whole group. It could also be used as part of an evaluative practice, e.g. at the conclusion of a professional learning session where teachers/learners could create or respond to questions related to their discoveries during the session/unit.

A variation: interactive huddles may pose a question to ask other groups or each group may huddle to generate a question for the leader.

PMI – plus-minus-interesting

A way to analyse ideas, information, topics for learning, suggestions or professional texts (written, visual, digital, aural). Teachers discuss in small groups/pairs and then write down (in a table or chart) what they believe to be the pluses, minuses and the interesting or impactful points on a particular aspect of a topic, text or experience. These reflective questions may be useful: What surprised you? Inspired you? What ideas/features appealed to you most? What was your 'a ha!' moment? What helped you learn? What do I do that helps you learn?

This strategy encourages exploration of new ideas or concepts and can also be used as a form of evaluation, reflection or self-assessment. PMI can be used in all circumstances and is also particularly helpful when there is a lot of information to be organised.

A variation: p*lus-minus-implications*: in this the teacher learners write or discuss the implications for what they have learnt for the future, for their learning, for their understandings for their practices, their student circumstances.

Three stars and a wish

A reflective activity, wherein individuals or groups list three specific 'good things' (the stars) about their learning and nominate one area in which they hope to improve (the wish).

Bundling

This strategy can be used to collate ideas on a given topic or text (written, visual, digital, aural) leading to groups of statements bundled according to sameness. It assists learners to make connections and to organise information (in paragraphs) after information is gathered for reporting back.

Roundtable

This is a cooperative structure in which one paper and one pen are systematically passed around the group. One person writes an idea and passes the paper and pen to the next person. This proceeds around the group. Allow think time and discussion time prior to passing the response sheet around the table group. After every two 'rounds' the roundtable process may be paused and additional thinking time allocated. It enables learners to consider another point of view, to build onto each other's ideas, extend their thinking and to compile thoughts, ideas, knowledge about any presented topic, text or statement.

Variation:

1. Rainbow writing: have each person have a different coloured writing tool (pen, pencil or texta) to use as the paper is passed around.
2. Simultaneous roundtable: each person has their own paper to start with (could be different colours) and each writes from the beginning of the time. The paper is passed around the group and each person adds their ideas on to the next paper (No Repeats) until the paper is returned to the original owner.
3. Surprise roundtable: each participant records one thing that 'surprised' them in the session or about the discussion topic or comments raised, the activity or the information given.

Mind mapping

Mind mapping is a way of organising and collate ideas onto paper. It is visual note taking and allows a great deal of information to be recorded onto a page. It shows relationships between various concepts and ideas. It uses a central image, key words, colours and symbols. Mind mapping can be used as a method for creating overviews, taking efficient notes, revising and creating a visual record of ideas. It can be used for mapping group discussions, information, negotiations, projects and group reviews or responses.

Brainstorming

This commonly used strategy produces many ideas on a given topic, concept or text (written, visual, digital, aural) in a relatively short space of time. All ideas are accepted without judgment in a brainstorming session.

Use the DOVE principle:

D: defer judgment – accept all contributions and evaluate later;
O: opt for original ideas – left field, unusual ideas/words may extend thinking;
V: vast numbers of ideas are best – narrow concepts down later;
E: expand by association – help an idea to grow and take off.

Use the FALL principle:

F: formulate a response;
A: articulate their ideas to the group;
L: listen, in turn, to other responses;
L: lengthen the thinking during the subsequent discussion by systematically building upon and elaborating the ideas of others.

Variations:

Think-Pair-Square: expert brainstorming requires individuals to brainstorm for one minute their own list of ideas. Individuals then make pairs and combine lists without repeating common ideas. Pairs join into fours to join their two larger lists. This method ensures that a contribution has been made from each person.

Popcorn: a form of brainstorming where a word, idea or question is 'throw' into a learning circle (either at the beginning or end of a lesson). Learners are requested to respond with the first thought that 'pops' into their heads. Importantly participants are encouraged to build upon concepts or connect to points raised by another person.

Chain reaction: groups of learners sit in a circle. The first person begins by asking a question on a nominated topic, concept, text or task. The second person answers the question and proceeds to ask a question of a third person. The process continues in a chain reaction until all members of the team have asked and answered a question relevant to the topic – it is an approach that is useful for winding up a session.

T- or Y-Chart

T-Charts are used to focus thinking and discussion about two aspects of learning. *Y-Charts* are used to elicit responses about three aspects of their learning.

Learners focus on an activity, concept or a situation. This strategy can be used in many situations, e.g. as an evaluative tool after a session, a task or activity, a text (written, visual, digital, aural), an inter-class visit, a PL session, etc. It is useful too, when a situational analysis is required, e.g. how does cooperative group work present in classrooms?

The chart is completed individually or in groups under the following headings:

- **Sounds like (T and Y):** What can you hear happening? A focus on sayings.
- **Looks like (T and Y):** What can you see happening? A focus on doings.
- Feels like (Y): How did you feel while taking part in the activity? A focus on relatings.

Three-step interview

Critical responses or questions are encouraged! This strategy can be used as a response task for any subject or session. It may be used at the beginning of a session as a 'getting to know you' activity. It is a simple scaffolding technique used to enhance both questioning and responding skills after reading a text or participating in a professional learning activity, and to elicit concerns or issues about a topic/discussion point.

'Literal or straightforward questions' elicit simple short factual responses. 'Critical questions' evoke detailed responses calling for higher order thinking responses such as reasons, justification, and explanations. Leaders may challenge learning teams to formulate a particular number of questions/comments (e.g. three 'critical' and three 'literal' questions).

The strategy provides scope for:

Paired learning:

1   Pairs are formed with a listener and speaker. A topic, text, activity or task is discussed and with consensus, questions are formulated.
2   Roles are reversed.
3   Pairs now join with another pair. Each person retells their partner's questions, concerns, issues or responses.

Group learning: teams may design 'critical' and 'literal' questions about their learning for another team to respond to; or write a provocative comment about the idea, issue or concern to which other groups have to respond.

Think, list, think, improve

As a group or individually, this strategy involves considering and recording the main features of the topic, or issues related to a text, topic, or educational problem. It involves:

i   thinking of ways to improve each feature, attribute, issue or aspect of learning, or solve a problem;
ii listing or recording ideas into some form of chart or grid;

iii thinking critically about what they need to work on and ways they can improve their learning, knowledge or understandings. This strategy can be used to develop creative solutions to problems or issues. Individually people think of as many options, solutions or opinions as possible. List them in a chart/poster/concept map;
iv individuals or pairs rethink, using time to improve ideas, practices, offer possible solutions to problems;
v report back to group considering all possible improvements.

Visual introduction

Aims to support learners activate prior knowledge by facilitating recall of experiences of a practice, activity, a problem, topic or known texts. This activity requires the learners, (prior to the session, reading, activity or task) to look at and consider the stimulus (visual stimulus that represents the topic or the problem, e.g. a picture, line drawing, meme, cartoon, photo, video clip, YouTube or diagram depicting the main idea of the session to follow). Learners write two or three sentence statements (or dot points) about what they anticipate would be the key problem, topic, issue raised and to be considered in the session. (Approx. five minutes.)
Procedure:

1 Leader selects an image depicting the main idea of the PL session to follow.
2 Instruct teachers to look at the picture for a few moments
3 Teachers write two or three sentences, statement or dot points about what they anticipate will be in the session.
4 Share their ideas (optional).
5 Engage in the session.

6Q4U (six questions for you)

Directed questioning significantly aids literal comprehension and recall of the main points of the lesson, text (written, visual, digital, aural) or task. This activity can help to activate prior knowledge or to recap learning at the end of a lesson.

Prior to learning session: This activity requires learners, prior to the learning or reading task (written, visual, digital, aural) to answer six questions focusing on important aspects of content of the lesson or text to follow.
Procedure:

1 Leader prepares six questions that focus on the important aspects of the content of the lesson or text.
2 Children are asked to write answers to each of these questions prior to proceeding to the text.
3 Children engage in the lesson or read or view the text.

4   Discuss the lesson or text in relation to what was new and what was already known.

Variations:

2Q4U: Use only one or two questions to guide the lesson or reading or viewing and build up over time, as students become experienced.

QAPX: Teams of four view or reflect on information provided by a text, video, lesson, internet search.... By rotating in the following manner:

Q: Person 1 Asks a QUESTION regarding the information
A: Person 2 supplies an ANSWER
P: Person 3 PARAPHRASES the answer
X: Person 4 EXPANDS on the answer with additional information

'Title talk' on task, topic or text

To activate learners' prior knowledge or experience before the learning experience, task, activity or reading.
Procedure:

1   Learners are given the title of the session, the text or the task or activity.
2   They are told to write down everything that they title made them think about. (Brainstorming – Learners are encouraged to allow their imaginations to run free in thinking about the title.)
3   They then share their ideas, in pairs, squares (four students). or as a whole class.
4   Children engage the lesson or read or view the text referring to their observations, predictions and interpretations as the lesson progresses.

The learning brain

This before and after strategy helps teachers identify what they already know about a topic, and to assist them consider what has been learnt after the session or even reading.

Materials: one piece of paper for each person (with a cloud shape drawn on if you like), coloured markers.

Procedure: Teachers:

1   are given a piece of paper (their 'BRAIN', a brainstorm cloud may be drawn on it or participants could draw a cloud in their notebooks);
2   are given the topic or title of the session or text to be read;
3   record everything they know about the particular topic;
4   read the text, participate in the session activities;
5   after the PL session, unit, task or text, they write any new information they have learnt (using the coloured markers) onto their 'brain';
6   discuss what was known and learnt.

TWL: think write learn: using a note book or learning log

Writing a response to a discussion, activity or text, a lesson, helps teachers reflect on new learning in a PL session and connect it with what they already know.

Learners may be asked to write about their professional learning processes (how they learnt), content, skills and knowledge (what they learnt) or implications (why this important and their opinions about it). You may ask teacher leaners to:

i   state the obvious
ii   go beyond the obvious
iii   establish connections
iv   express values
v   examine implications
vi   reflect critically on responses and learning processes; e.g. what was easy or hard? what remains a challenge? where to next? what else? how they learnt it?

Limits may be used; e.g. write 'three' things that were easy or supportive, and one thing that remains a challenge, issue, problem, concern.

Variation: learners may establish a THINK PAD in their notebook or learning logs to generate ideas/thoughts, etc. For example:

Language/discourse	*Solutions/answers/new ideas*
Questions/problems/issues	Connections (past/future practices)

This can be used in conjunction with a 'Think-Pair-Share' or 'Think-Pair-Square' Strategy.

In addition, learners may be able to identify questions for further study or clarification. Be solutions-focused – what are possible answers or solutions?

Jigsaw summary

Jigsaw summaries allow learners to collaboratively develop a précis of the main ideas contained in the session, activity or text. Each teacher develops a personal summary. Responses are compared and a combined 'master summary' is developed. It is focused on 'connected knowing' and allows all learners to make a start and contribute and to connect naturally with what has been taught/experienced. It encourages individual and group accountability, and caters for different learning styles and ages.

Process:

i   Form learning teams of three or four learners and allow participants time to think back over, re-read or re-view the session, concept, practice or text.
ii   Distribute 'jigsaw puzzle' worksheets on A4 or A3 paper.

iii Individuals write or draw six key points or images that summarise the main messages from the session, concept, practice or text.
iv Cut out individual jigsaws.
v Through discussion, each learning team arranges the individual pieces to create a 'best of' jigsaw representing the six best ideas/pictures of the group arranged in sequential order, paste pieces in place.
vi Each group member is to have at least one piece represented.
vii Teams join with another group to share
viii *Variations*: learning teams may design their own jigsaw proforma, complete a summary and have another group assemble the pieces. '*Pictorial Summaries*' with captioned headings could be constructed.

Why, Why, Why Chart

The *Why, Why, Why Chart* is a simple activity for building the vital habit of setting up a purpose for reading different types of text. It challenges students to think about various purposes for reading and viewing and to think critically about the subject matter or topic of each text (written, visual, digital, aural) or of the lesson.

Procedure: 1
Create a chart/handout/projected chart (such as the following samples). Feel free to modify the questions.
2 Make your presentation.
3 Have teachers fill in the chart as they read a engage with a point, consider an idea, etc.
4 Hold a discussion, raise issues to recorded answers, and synthesise what was learned, raised, considered, etc.

WHY might the main concept?	*WHY do we need to consider it?*	*WHY might the author/artist have written/created this particular text?*
WHY might I read/ view/ listen to this if I didn't (don't) have to?	**WHY did the author give the text this title?**	**WHY might the teacher want us to read/view/ create/listen to this?**

Variation: WH Chart: the focus WH questions may be centred on the topic of the learning.

WHAT are we learning about?	*How does this affect me, others the learning environment?*	*WHAT are the core issues we are discussing?*
WHY is this concept important to our student's lives? WHY do we need to know this?	**HOW does what we are talking about connect with other experiences or other issues?**	**WHY might the session leader want us to learn this? WHY might I learn this if I didn't (don't) have to?**

References

Edwards-Groves, C. (2003). On-task thinking: Reflective teaching and learning. In *On Task: focused literacy learning* (pp. 97–100). Newtown, Sydney, NSW: Primary English Teaching Association Australia (PETAA).

Appendix 3: Questions to guide evidentiary talk in professional learning conversations and for individual self-reflection

About planning:

- What information was gathered and used to identify student needs?
- How did you decide on the teaching focus?
- What is/was the desired outcome of this teaching session?
- What did you expect the class [or particular students] to be able to do able to do better? Improve on?
- How will you know if you have achieved your outcome?
- What criteria will you use to identify growth? Success?
- When and how will you gain this information during this lesson?

About the lesson:

- How did you introduce the lesson purpose?
- Was the new learning made explicit?
- Were students given the opportunity to review and practise previous learning?
- Was the lesson focus maintained?
- Were there opportunities for modelling/demonstrating, guiding learning and independent practice?
- How was the lesson concluded? Learning reviewed? How did the students indicate they learnt?
- What will the students need to learn next?

About students:

- Which students responded?
- How many students had an opportunity to respond?
- Did any students receive more opportunities than others? Why?
- Did students give extended responses? Were they supported to build onto and extend their responses?
- How were you supporting each child's learning?

About learning:

- What did the students learn from this lesson?
- What did the students learn today that s/he can use tomorrow?
- How can you help students develop this/transfer this [knowledge, strategy, process] in/to other learning contexts?
- How would/did the [action, behaviour] (observed) assist the student develop as a [reader, writer, learner]?
- Why is the [action, behaviour] (observed as above) important for student learning?
- How did you ensure the students achieved the learning goals? How do you know [what evidence do you have]?

About the interactions:

- Did you interact with each student? What was the purpose of that interaction? [to instruct? To mediate? To organise? To reprimand? To joke? To explain? To clarify? To repeat instructions? To review?]
- What tone?
- What was talked about? Did it serve the learning purpose?
- How much talking did you/the students do? Was that the intent?
- Were a range of grouping arrangements used [whole class, paired, small group, independent]?
- How did you foster student inquiry?
- Did you ask a range of questions? Literal questions? Inferential or thinking questions? Critical and analytic questions?
- Did you allow time for students to build 'chains of reasoning' [students building onto each other's thoughts, ideas, etc.]?
- Was the learning agenda interrupted to attend to behavioural and/or organisational agendas?

About assessment:

- What opportunities for assessment were taken? Were these made explicit?
- How was the information recorded?
- Did the assessment information add to that collected over time to provide comparative data?
- Did the design of the assessment task provide an equal opportunity of success for all student groups? Is it fair for all?
- Did the assessment information add to assessment data to provide a balance of information [teacher designed, external, in class]?
- Is the assessment linked to the teaching activity?
- Will the assessment information impact on future planning?
- Was assessment for learning? Of learning? As learning?

About teaching:

- What have you/we learned about [your] teaching?
- What will you work on/focus on next in your teaching?
- How did your/my analysis of the lesson help [you]?
- What else do we need to do? Know? Where can we find this information? Who will be responsible for seeking out the answers? The new knowledge?
- When will we meet again?

Appendix 4: Conversation transcription conventions

/	latched turns (intervening pause)
//	heard as interruption
[	said simultaneously; overlaps at this point
co:old	extended vowel or consonant
(4.0)	approximate length of pause in seconds
(( ))	transcriber's description, e.g. ((pause))
()	untranscribable
(mouse)	uncertain transcription
h, hh	aspirant sound
so-he-is	words said very quickly
ALONG	words read from text
?	interrogative or upward intonation question(prompt)
.	downward intonation (end of sentence)
, or -	minor pause
- -	longer pause
...	beginning or continuation of talk omitted
must	emphasis
T	teacher
S(s)	student(s)
J	initial of name of student speaking where this can be inferred

References

Source: Baker, C. and Freebody, P. (1989). *Children's First School Books*. Oxford: Basil Blackwell Inc.

Appendix 5: Supporting a dialogic approach: an example from the field – teacher reflection questions

The questions below are provided to provoke focused teacher reflection. They were used to facilitate teacher thinking about dialogic teaching during a long-term action research 'Researching dialogic pedagogies for high-impact literacy learning' (Edwards-Groves and Davidson, 2017). The questions provided a 'talk point' for the facilitator to provoke teacher thinking after a lesson observation and during a teacher 'de-brief' meeting. They were also used by the participating teachers to reflect on their own video-recorded lessons. Note: it is not necessary to address every question. Rather, questions should and can be adapted or added to, to meet individual purposes, professional learning goals or action research questions.

Ask teachers:

1 To what extent do you currently use a repertoire of dialogic pedagogies in your practice? What do you know? What have you tried? What are the challenging aspects of this?
2 How do you provide opportunities and time for students to:
   - sustain their thinking?
   - extend and deepen their thinking?
   - respectfully challenge the ideas and opinions of others?
   - think through and formulate ideas and opinions?
   - ask different kinds of questions?
   - control the learning dialogue with peers?
   - give learning-focused responses?
   - reflect on and review learning?
   - collaborate and cooperate?
   - listen actively?
   - practise and rehearse ideas?
   - articulate thoughts, ideas and opinions and rephrase if necessary?
   - give others time to think?
   - respond with and engage with the reasoning of others?
   - come to consensus?

- give and receive feedback respectfully?
- narrate; explain; instruct, receive, act and build upon answers; analyse and solve problems; speculate and imagine; explore and evaluate ideas; negotiate; discuss, argue, reason and justify? (adapted from Edwards-Groves, Anstey and Bull, 2014).

3 How do you ensure the students: can hear what others say? are listening to what others say? speaks at some point? What can you do differently today?
4 What else do you need to consider?

References

Edwards-Groves, C., Anstey, M. and Bull, G. (2014). *Classroom Talk: Understanding dialogue, pedagogy and practice*. Newtown, Sydney, NSW: Primary English Teaching Association Australia (PETAA).

Edwards-Groves, C. and Davidson, C. (2017). *Becoming a Meaning Maker: Talk and Interaction in the Dialogic Classroom*. Newtown, Sydney, NSW: Primary English Teaching Association Australia (PETAA).

Appendix 6: Learning together through action-oriented professional learning: a guide to collaborative peer coaching in the classroom setting

The following teacher learning practices form a basis for the 'cycles' or 'spirals' for action in professional learning. They aim to promote working collaboratively towards a *common goal*, to achieve individual and collective project goals, improved teaching, improved student learning practices and outcomes.

Aims

1   to problematise and refine teaching practice in order to improve student learning;
2   to make explicit what is known about teaching and learning;
3   to make covert practices overt (unexamined practices remain invisible and will not be improved);
4   to extend and challenge oneself to improve practice, extend and examine knowledge, skills and attitudes;
5   to engage in focused professional conversations and active learning with peers;
6   to trial learning with students in classrooms;
7   to consider new knowledge and ideas through focused professional reading.

The five practices for action-oriented professional learning:

1   plan
2   reflect
3   share
4   act
5   feedback.

Principles for cycles of plan-reflect-share-act-feedback

1   Successful peer coaching (in action research and site-based professional learning) depends on the relationship between the teachers. It is crucial to work with someone you trust.
2   Creating a trusting, supportive context that provides good dissonance (tensions and challenges) enables teachers to learn something new (without

tension teachers will not be extended and challenged to think differently, shift current stance or beliefs or consciously change practices).
3   Teaching is problematised.
4   Learning for all is valued and prioritised.
5   Committed practical action is prioritised and negotiated.
6   Understanding what each knows serves to support and extend professional relationships.
7   Knowledge and beliefs supported with contextual evidence enhances teacher learning.
8   Judgment is suspended to focus specifically on the targeted/negotiated areas for observation and change.
9   Ideas, beliefs and knowledge about teaching and learning are connected through focused professional conversations and reading.
10 Programme of action is manageable and achievable, observable and measurable.

Starting points: gathering information

1   A planful strategic, systematic approach, with well-established starting point (negotiated) is reflected at all stages; the process is structured detailed agenda and recorded minutes (and debrief notes).
2   What do we know? Gather information to gain perspective (professional learning partners may use reflective learning journals to record ideas, knowledge, action plans, thoughts, opinions, etc.) by asking:

   a   What is working well?
   b   What are my strengths and skills?
   c   What do I know?
   d   What are possible areas for growth and development?
   e   What are the challenges for me in this context?
   f   Why do I do the things I do? Say the things I say?

3   What do we want to know? Or do?

   a   Make informed hypotheses about perceptions and knowledge (accounting for context, background)
   b   Co-develop a tentative plan, ask teachers:

      i   What do you want to focus on?
      ii   What needs clarification?
      iii What do you want to change?

4   Negotiating support: targeting professional learning. Hold a *'pre-observation'* conference to discuss with peer learning partners:

   i   What will be the focal area for observation?
   ii   How will we go about this?
   iii Negotiating times and peer observations and debrief session.

Observing teaching: locating information

1. Teaching and focused (critical) observation (teachers may use videoed lessons).
2. Gathering evidence of change over time, ongoing, small steps to achieve the 'big picture'.

Focused professional conversations: interpreting, clarifying and analysing information

1. Debrief.
2. Collective focus; individual learning involves focused looking – what are we looking at? For?
3. An effective professional learning 'debrief' conversation has *five* essential features:

   a. It is tied to the specific learning event that has just occurred.
   b. It takes place in the context of the teachers' own work (as they attempt to learn about what they currently do, how they interact with the students, a specific technique or concept).
   c. It makes use of specific teacher and student actions, interactions and activity.
   d. It includes reciprocal reflection and constructive dialogue between professional peers as partners in learning.
   e. It results in new learning for both partners and a plan of action to improve teaching.

      i. What happened in relation to the observations focus area?
      ii. What worked well?
      iii. What did you learn?
      iv. Any other comments, observations?

Informed action: using information

1. Action: as a result of this session consider:

   a. What will be done next? What will we try?
   b. What timeframe?
   c. What/who do we need to seek out to extend knowledge skills and understandings?
   d. What will we need to learn next (conceptually) to reach another level of understanding, to take our learning further or to refine what we are doing currently?
   e. When will we next meet?

Reflections for the middle leader

1. Which of the five teacher learning processes do you currently do on a regular basis?

2 Which of the five teacher learning processes is the most challenging for you and why?
3 How can your team structure your project to ensure that all five processes are in place?
4 Is there another teacher learning process relevant to you and your professional learning?
5 How will you monitor your own and your team's progress and achievements?

Index

Page numbers in **bold** refer to figures, page numbers in *italic* refer to tables.

access 59
action-oriented professional learning 16, 109, 117, 119; aims 146; basis for 109; commitment 118; cycles 146–147; features 109–110; feedback 111; information gathering 147; leading 113–115; localised collaboration 110; participation 118; personal dimension of change 111–112; professional conversations 148; reflection 148–149; school-based 112–113; session planning 114–115; starting point 110; systematic development 110–111; teaching observation 148; and time 111; using information 148
action research xii, xv, 39–40, 83, 116; conditions for change 44–45; continuous development through 45–46; cycles 40, **40**, 45; initiating 42–43, 45; mathematical pedagogy case study 46–47; meetings case study 43–44; participation 47; physical education case study 40–42; reflection 45; sustaining 43
active listening 68–69
administrative work 7
agency 62
Ainscow, M. 2
assessment 78–79, 101–102; evidentiary talk questions 141
audio-video recording lessons 74

Basso, Keith 4
best practice 14, 35, 77, 79
Biesta, G. 79
blogging 124

capacity building 61
change: conditions for 44–45; evidence-based 40; leading 116–118; personal dimension 111–112; process 18; resistance to 117–118; sustainable xii
clarifying 117
classroom, definition 2
classroom discussion practices 104
classroom teaching, responsibilities xiv
classroom walkthroughs 84, 85, 100–101
collaboration 6, 96; building 42; and communication 7–8; localised 110
collaborative knowledge building 39–40
collegiality 42
commitment, shared 118
communication 6; and collaboration 7–8; and dialogic practice 64–65
communicative space 14, 56, 58, 59–60, 61, 94
communities of practice 14, 94
community building 59, 60–64, 94–95; key practices 96–99; and relational trust 99; sense of we 97–98; shared focus 98; and time 98–99
conceptual framework 14, 18–35
confidence 51
connectedness 61–62
continuous development 45–46
conversations: dialogic practice 64–65; focused 125–126, 148
Cox, R. 80
critical perspective 46–47
critical reflection 15
cross-school sessions 105–106
cultural-discursive arrangements 29, 33
curriculum development 6, 100

Darling Hammond, L. 109–110
data 15, 77–78, 78–79, 101–102
Davidson, C. 144
decision-making 74, 118
deep awareness 73
deprofessionalising 96
deputy principals 3
dialogic approach 144–145
dialogic learning 56–59, 72–74
dialogic practice 49, 56–74; the 3Rs 72–74; access 59; active listening 68–69; capacity building 61; challenging thinking 67–68; and communication 64–65; community building 59, 60–64; deepening thinking 67; dynamic 61; Early Years case study 60–64; engagement 66; feedback 71–72; focal point 66–67; guiding questions 70; inclusivity 59, 61; knowledge building 63; learning focused responses 71–72; opening communicative space 59–60, 61; physical arrangements 71; principles 59; professional learning conversations 65–74; shared responsibility 63–64; substantive dialogue 61–62; teacher agency 62; vacating the floor 71; wait time 69–70
dialogic talk moves 65
dialogue conferences 125–126
dialogue, definition 56
Dillon, D. 73
discourses 58
discussion: open 42; robust 61
distributed leadership 1
DOVE principle 133

ecologies of practice xv, 14, 20, 20–21, 31
education agendas 19
educational development 10, 39–40, 116
educational praxis 33
educational transformation, and trust 55–56
education complex of practices 20, **20**; middle leading and 22–28
education practice 4
education practices 4, 19–22, **20**, **21**, 31, 33, 95
education, purpose 4–5
education system 38
Edwards-Groves, C. 4, 5, 12, 55, 144
empathetic leadership 56
encouraging 117
engagement 66

enthusiasm 46
everyday practices, conduct of 32
evidence and evidence-informed development xi–xii, 15, 77, 77–91, 100–102, 111; analysis 103–105; assessment 101–102; collection 102–103; and data 77–78, 78–79, 101–102; evidence-base 80; evidence gathering 81–84; evidence-rich policy 79, 79–80; evidentiary talk questions 140–142; examples 83–84; fit for purpose 100–102; gathering 81–84; generation 102–103; importance 78; outward connections 105–107; in policy 79; and the practice landscape 80–81; qualities 81, 81–83; quality 80; recognisably worthwhile xv; transcripts 84–87, 89–91; using 102–105; worthwhile 81, 81–83
evidence-base 80
evidence-based change 40
evidence-informed dialogues 63
evidence-rich policy 79, 79–80
evidentiary talk 66–67, 67
executive leadership 7

facilitation 6–7, 43, 113–115
feedback 71–72, 111
feedup-feedback-feedforward loop 72, 111
Feez, S. 80
flexibility 106
focused observations 85
focused reflection 114–115
focus, shared 98
Friel, S. 72
Fullan, M. 2

generative leadership 11–12
generative pedagogical leadership xv
generative thinking 61
Glickman, C. 116, 117
good practice 10–11
Grootenboer, P. 38
guiding questions 70

happeningness 85
Hargreaves, A. 2
Hart, L. C. 73
hot site of education 39

immediacy 85
improvement, shared 111
inclusivity 59, 61

indigenous learners 46–47
intellectual engagement 33
intellectual trust 15, 51, *53*
interactional trust 15, 50, *51*
interactions, evidentiary talk questions 141
interdependent relationships 20–21
interpersonal trust 15, 50, *50*
intersubjective meaning making 28–29
intersubjective space 28–29
intersubjective trust 15, 50, *52*
inward-facing focus xv

journals 74, 124

Kemmis, S. xv, 4, 5, 11, 14, 20, 62, 78
knowledge building and development 63, 64

Lack, Peita 3
language 29, 58, 97
leadership: distributed 1; empathetic 56 executive 7generative 11–12; importance 1; pedagogical 19, 25–8, **27**, 28–30
leadership resources, focus xi
leading: with care 55; definition 2; practices 22; and teaching 6
learners, teachers as 12
learning environment 128
learning, evidentiary talk questions 141
learning logs 124, 137
learning partnerships 113
learning practices 14
learning resources and tools 128
Learning Support Team 107
lessons, evidentiary talk questions 140
lesson talk: student 127–128; teachers 126–127
lifeworlds 33
listening 63, 68–69, 117
listening stance 117
literature 1

management 3, 6–7
material-economic arrangements 30, 33
mathematical pedagogy 46–47
mathematics in high school case study 94, 95–96
meetings 7, 43–44, 98–99
metalanguage 63
middle leaders 1; classroom teaching responsibilities xiv; definition 2–3; dilemmas 47; impact xi; leadership position xiv; middleness 56; neglect xi; philosophical 9, 10; positional 9–10; practical 9, 10–11; praxeological 9–10, 11; responsibilities 2; role xiv–xv, 3, *3*, 59, 73, 114; support 39
middle leading 1–2; characteristics 9; complexity 26–27, **27**; dimensions of 6–8; education complex of practices and 22–28; influence 21, **21**; key idea 6; orchestrating 23–25; positioning 9–10, **9**; practice 5–8; purpose 4–5; shaping 22; understanding 8–12
middle management 3
middleness 56
misinterpretations 72
Morris, Dame Estelle 78–79
motivation xiv

ordinariness 32
organisational arrangements 3

participant direction-making 112
pedagogical change 34, 94, 95–96
pedagogical development 6
pedagogical leadership 19: site-based 25–28, **27**; spaces for 28–30
pedagogical practices 43
pedagogical praxis 34–35
pedagogical transformation xv
pedagogy development 44–45
peer coaching 146
peer observation 74, 84, 124–125
philosophical middle leaders 9, 10
physical education 40–42, 62
physical space-time 29, 30, 58
pictorial records 74
planning, evidentiary talk questions 140
position xiv
positional middle leaders 9, 9–10
practical middle leaders 9, 10–11
practice architectures xv, 22, 25, 57, 118; theory of 14, 18, 31–35, 110–111
practice-changing practice
practice-changing-practice xv, 15–16, 21–22, 109–120; Action-Oriented Professional Learning 109, 109–115
practice development 35, 77
practice landscape, and evidence 80–81
practice, theory of 14, 18, 31–35, 110–111
pragmatic trust 15, 51, *53*
praxeological middle leaders 9–10, 11
praxis 11
prefiguration of practices 32–33
principal, the 2, 3

problem-solving 74, 118
professionalism 97
professional learning and development 3, 6, 14, 19, 118: actioning 38; action-oriented 16; action research 39–46; commitment to 55; conditions for change 44–45; continuous 45–46; decision making 35; democratising 60–64; dialogic approach 56, 56–59; gold standard 109; importance 38, 100; leading 12, 39–40, 45; local level 39; orchestrating 23–25, **24**; physical education case study 40–42; reflection 45; school based 38–47; site 39; spaces for 28–30, 56; support 28, 39; vulnerability 55
professional learning communities 45, 63, 94, 95
professional learning conversations 86; the 3Rs 72–74; active listening 68–69; challenging thinking 67–68; deepening thinking 67; dialogic practice 65–74; engagement 66; evidentiary talk 66–67, 67; evidentiary talk questions 140–142; feedback 71–72; focal point 66–67; guiding questions 70; interdependency 68; learning focused responses 71–72; physical arrangements 71; vacating the floor 71; wait time 69–70
professional learning practices 22, 26, 31
professional learning space 28–30, 56
project-based learning 112
promising practice 14

quality teaching 19
questioning, improved 81–83
questions 104; evidentiary talk 140–142; guiding 70; probing 67; rich 81–83; self-reflection 126–129

reasoning 72
reciprocity 103
recognising 124
reconceptualising 68
recording equipment 87, **87, 88**
reflection 45, 73, 104–105, 111, 113; action-oriented professional learning 148–149; focused 74, 114–115, 130–139; questions 126–129
reflection strategies: 6Q4U (six questions for you) 135–136; brainstorming 133; bundling 132; dialogue conference 125–126; huddles 131; interactive 130–139; jigsaw summaries 137–138; the learning brain 136; learning logs – journaling – blogging 124; mind mapping 132; observe other teachers 125–126; pause button 130; peer observation and reflection 124–125; piggybacking 131; PMI – plus-minus-interesting 131; poster trail 130; recording lessons 124; roundtable 132; stop and ask time 130; teach and look back 123–124; think, list, think, improve 134–135; three stars and a wish 132; three-step interview 134; title talk 136; T- or Y-Chart 133–134; TWL: think write learn 137; visual introduction 135; whip around 131; Why, Why, Why Chart 138–139
reflective practice 58, 104–105
reflective practices 123–129; dialogue conference 125–126; learning logs – journaling – blogging 124; observe other teachers 125–126; peer observation and reflection 124–125; recording lessons 124; teach and look back 123–124
reframing 68
relational trust xv, 10, 49–52, *50, 51, 52, 53*; building 59; and community building 99; development case study 54–55; and educational transformation 55–56
researching and evaluation practices 22
resistance 117–118
responding 73
responses, learning focused 71–72
responsibility xiv, 1, 2, 35, 116; shared 63–64, 109
responsivity 106
reviewing 73
rich questions 81–83
right action 33
risk 117; recognising 111–112
Rönnerman, K. 12

school: definition 2; organisational arrangements 3; structures 97
school-based coherence 6
school-based development, long view 117
school formation and transformation 21–22, **21**
security 51
self-awareness 57
self-determination 4
self-development 4
self-expression 4

self-reflection 114–115, 126–129
semantic space 29
session planning 114–115
shared focus 98
shared responsibility 63–64
site-based education development 6, 27, 110
site-based pedagogical leadership 25–28, **27**
Smith, T. 11
social-political arrangements 30, 33
social practice, theory of 32–33
social space 29, 30, 58
spaces: for intersubjective meaning making 28–29; for pedagogical leadership 28–30; physical space-time 29, 30; semantic 29; social 29, 30
staff, reluctant 117–118
strategic development agenda 7
student lesson talk 127–128
students: evidentiary talk questions 140; learning practices 14, 19, 21, 31
substantial issues, addressing 116–117
substantive dialogue 61–62
substantive reasoning 63–64
supportive practices 28
sustainable change xii, 33
systematic inquiry, cycles of 112–3

teach and look back 74
teacher action research 14
teachers: agency 62; effectiveness 73; as learners 12; lesson talk 126–127; preparation 114; professionalism 118; reluctant 117–118; self-reflection questions 126–129
teaching 19; deep awareness 73; evidentiary talk questions 142; and leading 6; quality 19
teaching decisions 34–35
teaching practices 22

teaching space 56
teaching teams 97
technological practices 23–25, **24**
theory-of-practice-for-action 34–35
theory-of-practice-in-action 104, 110–111
theory, role of 32
thinking: challenging 67–68; deepening 67
time and time management 98–99, 111, 118
transcript conventions 87, 143
transcripts: acting on 90; analysis 89; benefits 85–86; conventions 87, 143; as evidence 84; pattern scanning 89; personnel 87; process 86–87, 89–91; as professional learning tools 84; reading 86, 89–90; recommendations 90; recording 87; recording equipment 87, **87, 88**; rereading 86; summary 90; themes 89; transcribing 87, 89
trust 10, 13, 14–15, 42, 49–56; building 59; commitment to 55; and community building 99; conditions for 51; development case study 52, 54–55; dialogic approach 56; dimensions of 15; and educational transformation 55–56; importance 99; intellectual 15, 51, *53*; interactional 15, 50, *51*; interpersonal 15, 50, *50*; intersubjective 15, 50, *52*; investment 54–56; maintaining 103; pragmatic 15, 51, *53*; relational 49–52, 54–56, 59, 99

wait time 69–70
we, sense of 97–98
whole school project case study 93–94, 95
wisdom 11
writing, focused 124
written logs 74